WHAT TO SAY

WHEN THINGS

GET TOUGH

WHAT TO SAY

WHEN THINGS

GET TOUGH

BUSINESS COMMUNICATION STRATEGIES FOR WINNING PEOPLE OVER WHEN THEY'RE ANGRY, WORRIED, AND SUSPICIOUS OF EVERYTHING YOU SAY

LEONARD S. GREENBERGER

New York   Chicago   San Francisco   Lisbon   London   Madrid   Mexico City
Milan   New Delhi   San Juan   Seoul   Singapore   Sydney   Toronto

1 2 3 4 5 6 7 8 9 0   QFR/QFR   1 9 8 7 6 5 4 3

ISBN   978-0-07-180643-5
MHID 0-07-180643-1

e-ISBN   978-0-07-180644-2
e-MHID 0-07-180644-X

McGraw-Hill Education books are available at special quantity dis-
counts to use as premiums and sales promotions or for use in corporate
training programs. To contact a representative, please e-mail us at
bulksales@mcgraw-hill.com.   .

This book is printed on acid-free paper.

Library of Congress Cataloging-in-Publication Data
Greenberger, Leonard S.
    What to say when things get tough : business communication
        strategies for winning people over when they're angry, worried, and
        suspicious of everything you say / by Leonard S. Greenberger.
        pages cm
    Includes bibliographical references.
(alk. paper) 1. Business communication. 2. Truthfulness and falsehood.
        3. Communication—Psychological aspects. I. Title.
    HF5718.G7394 2013
    658.4'5—dc23
                                                              2013002311

For my children, Brandon and Rachel,
the two most courageous people I know.

Contents

PREFACE

I recently celebrated my twentieth anniversary at the public relations firm where I work, Potomac Communications Group. We're a full-service public relations firm and help many types of clients communicate many types of messages to different audiences. In doing so, we've learned that the most effective techniques vary widely, depending to a large degree on the amount of trust and credibility the client has with the audience it's trying to reach. If we're promoting a consumer product or a conference for business executives, launching a new company, designing a new website, marketing a new energy-efficiency technology, or promoting a new series of publications to an association's membership, we can help our clients communicate as trusted peers and valued information sources. Those same clients need a very different style when they address something that represents even the perception of a threat to the audience—to the audience's health, environment, financial viability, and so on. They must change the very way they communicate—how they stand and dress, whether they should make jokes or smile, and how they hold their arms, tell stories, present information, or answer questions—everything. A business professional in even the most benign industries today must be prepared to shift from one style and set of strategies, skills, and techniques to the other at a moment's notice.

Not long after I started with the company, one of our founding partners attended a conference in Texas on communicating in tough situations. Although the conference focused on energy issues, the organizers invited a senior communicator with a soft-drink company to be the luncheon speaker. She described the challenges associated with the "cola wars"—the marketing battle between cola giants Coke and Pepsi, and their smaller competitors. After lunch the attendees were all saying to one another how refreshing it would be to talk about bubbly, friendly issues like cola instead of much more formidable risks such as air and water pollution. Then they learned that the cola executive had to leave early to fly home because of a breaking news story about someone tampering with some of her company's soft-drink bottles and some dangerous substances that had been found inside. It was a stark reminder that *everyone* in *every* industry and company today needs to be prepared, all the time, to break through and win people over in very tough situations. It can happen to anyone at a moment's notice.

While the circumstances vary, tough situations have one crucial element in common: traditional communication strategies that work perfectly well in "normal situations" prove to be ineffective. When the people with whom you're communicating are angry, worried, and suspicious of everything you say, you need to employ different skills and techniques to win them over.

That sort of challenge fascinated me from day one.

Like any young professional, I spent a lot of time during my first few years absorbing knowledge and expertise from people much more experienced and wiser than I was. These included my own colleagues, of course, as well as some of the firm's clients. I also learned as much as I could from outside experts, including Dr. Vincent Covello, director of the Center for Risk Communication in New York City; Dr. Albert Mehrabian, currently professor emeritus of psychology at the University of California at Los Angeles; Dr. Peter Sandman, founder of the Environmental Communication Research Program at Rutgers University and now a private consultant; and Dr. Paul Slovic, a psychology professor at the University of Oregon.

As I gained experience, I began to build on the theory and practice I had soaked up in those early years with lessons learned and skills and techniques developed through hands-on work with clients. My colleagues and I learn something new every time we help guide a client through a tough situation, and we constantly hone our strategy and approach. Eventually, I became enough of an expert that organizations began inviting me to speak about communicating in tough situations. I've traveled all over the country, sometimes training a handful of people and sometimes presenting to hundreds. All told, I would guess that my colleagues and I have worked with close to ten thousand people over the years.

It was on one of these trips, to the California Society of Association Executives' annual conference in April 2010 in Long Beach, California, that I began the journey that culminated in this book. In this particular instance, the audience was small, about 30 people. I gave my standard presentation on breaking through and winning people over (though I didn't call it that yet), and I got a nice round of applause at the end. I went a little over my allotted time, as usual, and most of the attendees shuffled out the door quickly to get to their next sessions.

As I was packing my bag, one woman approached me. That's not unusual. People often come up after I speak to ask quiet questions they didn't want the whole room to hear.

"I just want to thank you for an informative presentation," she said, shaking my hand. "It was very helpful. And I was wondering, where can I buy your book?"

The question startled me. I've given scores of similar presentations for thousands of people. She was the first who ever asked me about a book.

"Well, thank you," I replied. "I'm glad you enjoyed it. But I'm afraid I haven't written a book."

She smiled and shook my hand. "That's too bad," she said, turning away. "You should."

On the long flight home to Washington, D.C., that afternoon, I decided she was right.

My firm typically works with high-ranking corporate executives, government officials, and military officers, preparing them to deliver or react to bad news or to address false allegations and misinformation. But the strategies, skills, and techniques we teach apply in any tough situation when an audience, whether one person or many, is angry, worried, and suspicious of everything you say. And not just in professional settings. These lessons come in handy in personal relationships, too. I've often thought that just about everyone would benefit from our training, and after talking to the woman in Long Beach, I realized that a book would give me a way to reach more people than I ever could by crisscrossing the country and speaking to relatively small groups. So, as I was cruising at 35,000 feet above the Rocky Mountains, I took out my laptop and began to write.

This book is intended to be a very practical, hands-on primer that anyone who faces an angry, worried, and suspicious audience can use to break through and win the audience over. You'll find a little theory, but mostly real-life examples based on my own work and that of my colleagues. I've changed names and other specifics, because I want to respect my clients' confidentiality, but every story is real and true.

I tell the people I train and the clients I serve that they can't expect to become experts in winning people over after just one training or strategy session. The same is true for this book. Even if you read it cover to cover, which I hope you will, you won't become an instant expert at winning people over in tough situations. That takes time, practice, and experience. But with careful preparation and proper application of the strategies, skills, and techniques discussed in the pages to follow, you'll be on your way. I hope you'll keep the book on a shelf in your office or at home and refer to it again and again.

And to the anonymous attendee at the 2010 CalSAE annual conference who launched me on this journey, I just want to say, "Thank you."

ACKNOWLEDGMENTS

While my name is on this book, many people made it possible. The list begins with my colleagues at Potomac Communications Group, and right at the top is Russ Dawson. Though I earned a master's degree in journalism and worked as a reporter for more than two years before joining the firm, I knew almost nothing about public relations when I came on board. Russ took me under his wing and showed me the ropes. More than anyone else, he deserves credit for developing my firm's approach to communicating in tough situations when people are angry, worried, and suspicious of everything you say. His ideas and thoughts flow through every page.

I also owe a huge debt of gratitude to the two people who hired me, the firm's founding partners, Ellen Lepper and Bill Perkins. Ellen passed away many years ago, but I hear her sage advice and wise counsel echo in my mind at least once a day. Bill is the only person who read every word of the manuscript before I submitted it to McGraw-Hill, and he helped me find my voice and provided insightful edits and comments at every step along the way.

My other partners, Mimi Limbach, Andy Hallmark, and Nora Howe, deserve credit, too. Many of the anecdotes I've shared are based on Mimi's and Andy's experiences with clients. All three gave me the time and space I needed to research and write and kept the trains running while I was locked in my office for hours and days at a stretch. Not to mention the fact that Nora saved me when computer viruses attacked my laptop and threatened to destroy many hours of hard work—twice.

Several members of our staff helped as well. I especially want to thank Barbara Longsworth, who created all the original illustrations, and Nathan Petrillo, who edited several early chapters, as well as Casey Orr and Jacquelynne Carpenter, who read through piles of books and papers and sifted out just the right quotes or facts I needed.

On a more personal note, this book never would have happened without the assistance and encouragement of my cousin and coagent, Wendy Paris. More than anyone else, Wendy convinced me I could do it and kept me sane while I did. She also edited and re-edited my original book proposal and introduced me to my other coagent, Andrew Stuart, who made the connection with McGraw-Hill.

Speaking of which, the team at McGraw-Hill was incredibly professional and skillfully guided me through the entire publishing process. My thanks to Donya Dickerson, Scott Rattray, Pattie Amoroso, and Lisa Schweickert, as well as to what I'm sure are many others whom I didn't get to meet but helped to make this book happen.

Finally, I want to thank my parents, Judie and Shelly, for inspiring me to succeed and supporting me when I've failed. And my kids, Brandon and Rachel, who put up with a lot of boring weekends while Dad sat at the dining room table and wrote.

INTRODUCTION

I did not have sexual relations with that woman.

—PRESIDENT BILL CLINTON

In February 2012, Mimi Alford published an autobiography in which she described her sexual affair with President John F. Kennedy during her time as a White House intern. The book got a little attention, but it was hardly major news. After all, Alford had not been President Kennedy's only dalliance. Judith Campbell, the reputed girlfriend of Chicago crime boss Sam Giancana, also claimed to have had an affair with the president. Others, both alleged and confirmed, include Jacqueline Kennedy's press secretary, Pamela Turnure, movie stars Angie Dickinson and Kim Novak, and perhaps most famously, Marilyn Monroe.

At the time, the general public knew none of this. While several close Kennedy confidants, as well as a number of reporters, have admitted that they were aware of the president's indiscretions, they chose to remain silent. We only learned of the president's indiscretions many years later, well after his tragic assassination in Dallas.

Fast-forward 35 years.

From 1995 to 1997, another young, charismatic president engaged in a sexual affair with a White House intern. When the news broke in January 1998, it ignited a media firestorm that lasted more than a year. Reporters deluged us with endless information about President Bill Clinton's relationship with Monica Lewinsky. We were spared no detail, and the president suffered the embarrassment of impeachment for lying about the affair.

You might wonder why I would begin a book about breaking through and winning people over when they're angry, worried, and suspicious of everything you say with, well, sex. In this case, it's not because sex sells. The fact that these presidents' ethical lapses happened to be sexual in nature is really beside the point. What's far more relevant is the way society, and particularly the media, reacted to two very similar stories that took place more than three decades apart. In the first instance, society did not discover the president's indiscretions at the time, precisely because reporters who knew about them decided that the public had no need—or even right—to know about them. By the time President Clinton came to office, the Kennedy-era view had become an antiquated notion at which most reporters would scoff (see Figure I.1). If the president did something, it was news. And if he did something wrong, it was *big* news.

What happened? Simply put, society changed, beginning not long after President Kennedy's death. The 1960s gave rise to the civil rights and environmental movements. Vietnam split the country in two, and unlike their parents and even grandparents, the up-and-coming Baby Boom generation had no compunction about challenging the nation's leaders on the justification for or conduct of the war. In my mind, the Watergate scandal marks the end of this fundamental upheaval in the relationship between people in positions of authority and those they sought to govern or control. Ever since, as a society, we have

FIGURE I.1 What a Difference 35 Years Can Make

Presidents Kennedy and Clinton both engaged in sexual affairs with young White House interns. Though aides and friends knew, Kennedy's affair went unreported for almost five decades. Clinton's affair ignited a media firestorm that lasted more than a year and ended with his impeachment. This one high-profile example demonstrates how people today, including reporters, are much more skeptical and much less respectful of authority. It helps to explain why you need new strategies, skills, and techniques to break through and win people over in tough situations when they're angry, worried, and suspicious of everything you say. And that's true whether we're in the office, on vacation, or at home with relatives and friends.

been much less trustful and much more skeptical of our leaders, and not just in the areas of politics and government. The same is true in almost every field: business, the military, sports, entertainment, and even religion. And I see no sign that this trend is going to reverse itself. We continue to be rocked by scandals that lower the level of trust and credibility our society affords its leaders. The banking scandals that helped bring about the Great

Recession. Martha Stewart and her conviction and imprison-ment for insider trading. Tiger Woods and his extramarital affairs. The Catholic Church's attempt to cover up pedophilia by far too many of its priests. The Penn State scandal. I could go on and on.

I'm not a sociologist, and this book is by no means about sociology. I mention this change in the way we treat people in positions of authority to help illustrate why we find ourselves needing to communicate in tough situations so much more often today. People are more likely to be angry, worried, and suspicious in large part because they are less trusting and find their leaders to be far less credible than the generations that came before them, and because they feel empowered to fight back when they feel risks are being imposed on them. We don't necessarily need to understand why we've arrived at this place, only that we are here. This is the context in which we operate as communicators, whether we're at the office, stuck in traffic, or engaging with our families. We can't change the context. We can only accept it and change how we approach tough situations in twenty-first-century America, employing new strategies, skills, and techniques to break through and win people over.

That is what this book is about.

Let me say a few words about what this book is *not* about. This is not a book about crisis communications, though the strategies, skills, and tactics we'll discuss are very applicable in crisis situations. When an organization, or an individual, is presented with a sudden crisis and faces a tough situation and an angry, worried, and suspicious audience, what we'll discuss in this book will definitely help. But crises require responses that go beyond communications. In that sense, you might view this book as merely a chapter in a larger volume on the much broader subject of crisis communications.

Nor is this book about risk communication, a specialized field of study that gave rise to most of the strategies we're going to discuss. We'll look at this relatively new and immensely important new science in Chapter 1. As you'll see, the field largely grew out of research into the best ways to communicate about environmental and public health risks in a less trustworthy and credible world—risks that include everything from chemicals in food to emissions from power plants. What my firm has done is to take the tools and techniques rooted in the science of risk communication and apply them beyond these areas to everyday business situations.

The anecdotes I'll share along the way are based on real-life experiences that my partners and I have had working with clients over the years. While they include traditional "risk scenarios," such as trying to build a controversial power line or explaining a toxic spill, I'll also cite examples involving an organization forced to terminate its highly regarded chief executive officer because of financial impropriety, as well as a doctor thrust into a potentially hostile media interview simply because he happened to be attending a meeting when a controversial local issue hit the front pages. We've even called upon the strategies, skills, and techniques needed to communicate effectively in tough situations when my firm has had to dismiss our own employees for poor performance.

I also describe many situations involving prominent political and business leaders. They make easy targets, and, unfortunately,

I have no limit to the number of poor performances in tough situations that I can cite. These examples are also useful because they're widely known and therefore broadly relatable. Very few people get to see my partners and me when we work with clients. Millions saw BP's chief executive officer Tony Hayward attempting to defend himself in the wake of the big Macondo oil spill in April 2010 in the Gulf of Mexico and Sarah Palin's disastrous interview with *NBC News* reporter Katie Couric during the 2008 campaign (when she couldn't name a newspaper she read regularly and cited Alaska's proximity to Russia to burnish her foreign-policy expertise). These make big news, but tough situations play out in millions of offices and homes across the United States and around the world every day of the year.

That brings me to my last point about what this book is not: purely a business book. While *What to Say When Things Get Tough* is based on my firm's experience working with business clients, the strategies, skills, and techniques we'll discuss are eminently applicable in personal relationships as well. I've used them successfully at times myself, helping to diffuse tough situations with, for example, several women in my life. Of course, I've also tried to apply them and failed miserably. And that is why I won't dwell on personal relationships in this book. I don't pretend to be an expert in this field, and the strategies, skills, and techniques required to break through and win people over work best when you as a communicator have no emotional relationship with an audience.

As we'll see, when people are angry, worried, and suspicious of everything you say, they are almost by definition very emotional. We have to be careful about our own emotions in tough situations. I recently came across an article by Christina Miranda, a fellow PR expert and author of *The Voice of Reason in Marketing*, a blog at http://redpointspeaks.com, in which she offers advice on how to deliver bad news and summarizes the need to avoid emotion in tough situations. Miranda writes, "Come to terms with [information] you must deliver so you don't bring any [negative] emotional energy to the communication. Your audience will take its cue from your approach, and if you're defensive, nervous, weepy, or angry, it will only fuel their negative response."

We'll explore in later chapters how people filter everything you say and do in tough situations. For now, when it comes to communicating with loved ones, I'll leave it to you as a reader to find elements and passages that make you think, "Hey, I'm going to try that the next time I get into a big fight with my significant other." Just keep in mind that personal relationships are fraught with far more complicated challenges than business relationships because of the emotional connections that exist between us and the people we love.

THE DEMISE OF TRUST AND CREDIBILITY

Let's return to the changes in society illustrated by the reactions to the twin presidential scandals and look more closely at what happened in the span of those 35 often chaotic years. (And please do not read any partisanship into the fact that these two leaders happen to be Democrats; this is a decidedly nonpolitical book, as is my firm. We'll pick on Republican politicians as well.) Because of what has changed over the last 40 or 50 years, people are more skeptical and less trusting. More of us than ever before find our-selves in situations where our audience is angry, worried, and suspicious—in other words, tough situations. Not long ago, the techniques discussed in this book came into play only in really nasty situations—during big environmental disasters or political scandals, for example. Now a tough situation can arise almost anywhere at any time: in the office, on the subway, even at home. Whereas these techniques were once the province of corporate CEOs and other true authority figures, today everyone needs to understand and use them. We are all authority figures now.

In early-1960s America, one simply did not openly discuss the private lives of presidents or of just about anyone else, for that matter. Most Americans accorded their leaders a high level of trust and respect simply by virtue of the jobs they held and the hard work it took to get them. Relatively few questioned author-ity figures, not even the reporters who covered them. Consider one more example from the presidential archives: Shortly after assuming the presidency, Lyndon Johnson met with a group of reporters for a briefing on his goals for the new year of 1964. According to Hal C. Wingo, who helped launch *People* magazine and was then working for *Life* magazine, the president leaned forward as the briefing was about to end and said,

> One more thing, boys. You may see me coming in and
> out of a few women's bedrooms while I am in the White
> House, but just remember, that is none of your business.

They obeyed. Wingo related this anecdote in an April 23, 2012, letter to the editor to *New Yorker* magazine. The letter concluded: "[Johnson] had just made it clear that he wanted the same cover the press had given Kennedy, and the rules were stacked in favor of the President. We knew that he was right about the rules, at least for then."

Imagine Bill Clinton trying that in 1998, when Michael Isikoff of *Newsweek* was ready to break the Monica Lewinsky story (which actually came out first on the *Drudge Report* website). No one questioned whether the private life of the president was indeed private. Reporters fell over themselves trying to cover the story. They looked at it from every angle and left no detail unreported.

Many factors played into the different ways that reporters covered presidents' indiscretions in these examples, but they illustrate how the erosion of trust and credibility accorded to authority figures affects us as communicators. (Of course, President Clinton didn't help his case when he uttered the now-infamous line I used to open this Introduction. But even if he hadn't lied about the affair, society's reaction likely would have been just as explosive. As we move on, keep President Clinton's quote in mind. We'll come back to it again in Chapter 6.)

THE PARAMOUNT IMPORTANCE OF TRUST AND CREDIBILITY

The "gotcha politics" of the last two decades, in which politicians seek to tear down their opponents personally rather than to counter the merits of their arguments, is an extension of this erosion of trust and credibility. It has affected every aspect of society: each time respected national figures or institutions behave unethically or immorally, they chip away another piece of the trust and credibility that we used to confer on authority figures.

That's a big problem for anyone who hopes to break through and win over people when they're angry, worried, and suspicious.

More than ever before, trust and credibility are a communicator's most precious qualities. They're also ephemeral. They're essential but elusive. They're difficult to measure or define. They're hard to obtain but easy to lose. We may have them in some situations or on certain topics but not others.

For our purposes, it's enough to know that establishing ourselves as trustworthy and credible sources of information is the most crucial prerequisite for successful communication. This is true for presidents, doctors, lawyers, movie stars, and journalists, as well as for bosses, employees, peers, friends, siblings, and significant others—in other words, for everyone.

Most of the time, in normal situations, we don't have to work very hard to establish and maintain trust and credibility. That's largely because most everyday interactions do not take place with people when they're angry, worried, and suspicious. Take our relationship as author and reader, for instance. Presumably, as the author of this book, I hold a certain level of trust and credibility in your eyes. I can think of several reasons why that's (hopefully) the case:

▶ I've been a professional communications consultant for more than 20 years, so you assume I have a certain level of expertise based on what I've learned and accomplished during my career.

▶ If you read the author's blurb, you learned that I have a bachelor's degree in communications and a master's degree from Northwestern University, one of the country's most highly regarded journalism schools.

▶ It helps, too, that McGraw-Hill agreed to publish this book. If they didn't think I knew what I was talking about, or if what I had to say wasn't important or valuable, they wouldn't have paid me to write it. That's an example of third-party credibility, and in Chapter 2, we'll talk more about how it can help you break through and win people over.

▶ You don't perceive me to be any sort of threat to you or to anyone you care about. After all, what's the worst that can happen, now that you've bought the book? You don't like what I have to say, and you toss it in the trash. Maybe you'll be upset that you wasted your money, but no one will come to any real harm.

Normally, we also benefit from a previously established level of trust and credibility when we interact with coworkers, neighbors, family, and friends. In these situations, we tend not to worry about trust or credibility. It's assumed, already built into the relationship. In other words, we've already won those people over.

That doesn't mean we don't have to work to *maintain* trust and credibility in normal situations. As an author, I may lose them if you decide I don't know what I'm talking about. It could even happen in person if you bring this book to a signing and I say something you don't like. Or I show up late. Or I leave before I sign your book. The same is true in our personal lives.

Under normal circumstances, you may have a great deal of trust and credibility with your significant other. But if you do something wrong and get into a fight, those qualities can evaporate quickly—and take a long time to restore. Your employees may think you're very trustworthy and credible until you reprimand them. Or even worse, let them go. Or make a big mistake. You may have earned a great deal of trust and credibility with your boss, until you screw up an assignment.

In large part because of the steady erosion of the level of trust and credibility that we accord our leaders, our ability to win people over is much harder today in tough situations. That's particularly true when we are viewed as authority figures.

In tough situations, the normal rules of communication we follow and experience in our everyday interactions with family, friends, and colleagues no longer apply. We have not earned any trust and credibility with audiences who have these feelings; instead, when we initiate communication, we possess very little, if any, of these precious qualities. When people are angry, worried, and suspicious, you must *earn* their trust and establish credibility. You have to do it immediately and instantaneously, and then maintain trust and credibility throughout the interaction and even after it ends. If you don't, nothing you say or do will inform, educate, or persuade anyone of anything. It may sound harsh, but as a communicator, you will have failed.

In the end, I wrote this book with one goal in mind: to empower you to establish and maintain the trust and credibility you'll need in tough situations. When people don't trust you. When they're angry about something that you've done to them or that they perceive you've done to them. When they're worried because they're concerned or afraid. When they're suspicious, because they think you only have your own best interests in mind.

Once you've finished the book, and with lots of practice, careful preparation, and proper application of the strategies, skills, and techniques we're going to discuss, you'll be well on your way to being ready to break through and win people over in the toughest situations.

Before we get started, I want to share one final thought that I always tell the people I train. The strategies, skills, and techniques you'll learn in this book can be used not only to educate and inform but also to mislead and manipulate. I trust that you'll use them for the good purposes they are intended because to do otherwise would be highly unethical and patently immoral—and can backfire and destroy your trust and credibility forever.

Now, with that important admonition out of the way, we'll start with a quick review of the science that gave rise to these strategies, skills, and techniques.

THE SCIENCE BEHIND THE ART

To be persuasive we must be believable; to be believable we must be credible; to be credible we must be truthful.

—EDWARD R. MURROW,
AMERICAN BROADCAST JOURNALIST

Implementing the strategies you'll need to win over angry, worried, and suspicious people involves a mixture of art and science. In this book, we're going to focus mostly on the art: how to tell a story; how to weave your messages into responses to difficult questions; how to use verbal and nonverbal cues to build trust and credibility; how to avoid traps and escape from them if you fall in. One of the messages I hope to drive home is that communicating in tough situations is in large part a performance, similar to what a singer does on stage or an athlete does on a playing field. No professional performer would appear publicly without weeks, months, and even years of practice, preparation, and rehearsal. Nor should you.

Still, the strategies, skills, and techniques we're going to cover in this book are based on real laboratory and field research, and I find that it's helpful for my clients to understand a little about the science—and history—behind the art of winning over people in tough situations. Some experts trace the science all the way back to the emergence of modern governments in Western Europe and the first stirrings of the Industrial Revolution. We're not going to go back quite that far.

For our purposes, we only need to return to where we were in this book's Introduction: the 1960s. As the erosion of trust and credibility took hold following that turbulent decade, average people began to demand a bigger role in making decisions. New laws, beginning with the landmark Clean Air Act of 1963, provided for citizen lawsuits for the first time. Over time, the public increasingly flexed its new muscles, and by the late 1970s and early 1980s, a considerable amount of power had shifted demonstrably from people in positions of authority to people generally.

Let me illustrate the point with a real-life example. My firm recently worked with a utility that wanted to build a new high-voltage power line. In the 1960s, our client would have spent a lot of time preparing detailed engineering and economic studies designed to convince state regulators that the line was needed and that they had outlined the most economical route. They would have exerted very little, if any, effort to persuade people who lived in the communities where the line would run that they should be allowed to build it. And why would they? The chances that anyone would complain or oppose the new line were practically nonexistent 50 years ago. And even if someone tried to stop it, the chances of success were essentially nil. If utility and government experts agreed that the line needed to be built, who were everyday citizens to question their judgment?

That's not the way it works today. The United States became prosperous enough that many people could afford to be concerned about issues other than economics. The most efficient and economic path for a power line wasn't persuasive if it ran through a park, or wetland, or picturesque countryside, or—later, because of fears associated with exposure to electric and magnetic fields (EMF)—near a school or through a residential neighborhood. Health and safety issues, environmental protection, even aesthetics had to be considered, and so did public opinion. A proposed new facility doesn't even have to be "dangerous" in the traditional sense to generate opposition. In this era of ultra-NIMBYism (where NIMBY is shorthand for "not in my backyard"), trying to build new parks or day care centers can become contentious. Right now, my own neighborhood is up in arms over a developer's plans to build a new apartment building on a piece of property that has been vacant for decades. Nor does it have to be about building something. Even *removing* facilities can be controversial. I recently attended a meeting where a dam safety expert expressed surprise at the tenacity with which a local community fought his company's plans to demolish an old, crumbling, essentially worthless dam.

Companies can't ignore people, nor can they expect people to simply accept their word for *anything*. Our utility client had to spend as much time engaging and communicating with people in communities all along the proposed 200-mile line as they did with state regulators. My firm facilitated more than a dozen public meetings, developed a whole family of materials to describe and explain the project, and set up a website dedicated to informing and educating local residents and providing them with multiple opportunities to participate in the process and express their views. For the utility to get permission to build the line, breaking through and winning over people who lived and worked near the proposed route was just as important as convincing regulators that the line was necessary from an economic standpoint. And I can tell you that many of those people were plenty angry, worried, and suspicious. I'll finish this story, and reveal whether the line got built, in the next chapter.

The Rise of Risk Communication

By the 1980s, people in positions of authority within government and industry began to realize that the old way of doing business wasn't working anymore. They needed new communication strategies, skills, and techniques to succeed in a world where they could no longer simply tell people what they were about to do—where, instead, they had to address people's concerns and fears in order to win them over.

Partially in response to this need, researchers developed a new field of study known as "risk communication," a whole new science now taught in colleges across the country and featured in lectures, conferences, and peer-reviewed journals. Many definitions of risk communication exist, but I particularly like one published in a Joint United Nations Food and Agriculture Organization/World Health Organization Expert Commission report, because it's short and succinct: "Risk communication is the exchange of information and opinions concerning risk and risk-related factors among risk assessors, risk managers, consumers and other interested parties."

Simply put, risk communication provides rules and guidelines that allow experts or those in positions of authority to help people assess, understand, and properly respond to threats both real and perceived. The strategies we're going to cover in this book are rooted in those rules and guidelines.

Risk communication traces its roots back to the progressive movement of the early twentieth century, when public-health professionals first began to define health risks associated with sanitation and food safety and to educate people about how to reduce those risks. The Second World War accelerated this "professionalization of risk" as policy makers incorporated risk assessment and analysis into military decision making. By the 1960s, experts understood enough about risk analysis and management to incorporate the concepts into laws and regulations. Indeed, the landmark legislation of the 1960s and 1970s that first empowered people with a voice in environmental policy depended on those concepts. Communication experts picked up on this new understanding of risk assessment and analysis and began to develop new ways to communicate with people newly empowered to question and oppose those in positions of authority. So in a sense, the trends that emerged during the 1960s both created the need for new communication strategies, skills, and techniques and gave rise to the science that ultimately provided them.

Today, we have a very strong understanding of how people perceive and assess risk when they're angry, worried, and suspicious; what factors influence those perceptions and assessments;

when and how emotional thinking trumps rational thinking; and how all of that plays into whether people consider a specific source of information to be trustworthy and credible. We'll explore all of these issues in Chapter 4.

As the science of risk communication has evolved based on new research findings, so has the way people in positions of authority have applied the rules and guidelines rooted in it. In *Solutions to an Environment in Peril*, edited by Anthony Wolbarst and originally published in 2001, experts Vincent Covello and Peter Sandman describe three stages that government and industry leaders have passed through as they have sought to apply the principles of risk communication (the labels for each stage are mine):

1. Ignore
2. Explain
3. Engage

Let's take a closer look at each stage.

Ignore

Before 1985, Covello and Sandman argue, most leaders simply chose to disregard the emerging principles of risk communication and continued to avoid communicating about risk. This always had worked before, when everyone assumed experts knew best, people had little recourse to challenge them, and leaders were slow to understand that the context in which they were attempting to communicate had changed. Some significant events during the early 1980s, including the cancellation of several major infrastructure projects in the United States due to citizen opposition and the whole world's outraged reaction to the Union Carbide chemical spill in Bhopal, India (which killed thousands), made it increasingly clear that ignoring risk communication principles was no longer an option.

It's important to note that, while government and industry leaders may not have been communicating effectively with the public, their lack of communication doesn't mean they ignored risks associated with their actions. They still took seriously the need to protect public health and the environment. They just didn't think they had to, nor did they know how to, communicate about it.

Explain

Once it became clear that willful ignorance didn't work anymore, many government and industry leaders tried to explain risk better. Under the theory that if people only understood the nature of a given risk, they would accept it (and by implication, leave the experts alone to do as they pleased), they began to share risk data with the public more often. A better understanding of the factors that influence risk, including benefits, fairness, and control, allowed those in positions of authority to persuade people to accept risks that they greatly feared but that represented very minimal threats.

The mantra then was to "educate" the public. Just give people the facts, and that will win them over. Many government agencies and virtually every industry spent a lot of effort and money on educating—rolling out numbers and studies and facts in every form imaginable. It was definitely better than ignoring the public, but not by enough to really make a difference. Simply sharing facts and information didn't win people over. The public still rarely fell in line.

Engage

While Covello and Sandman believe many government and industry leaders remain stuck at the "explain" stage, they also believe others have moved on. What began as no communication and then moved on to one-way communication has become two-way interaction. Leaders began trying to engage members of the public, even those who were very angry, worried, and suspicious. These leaders accepted Sandman's belief that people perceive risk as a function of "hazard" (danger) and "outrage" (fear). To be effective, experts not only had to explain the danger but also reduce the fear. To do so, they had to give members of the public an opportunity to share their concerns and be heard, and, most of all, they had to address not just the facts but also the emotions the audience is feeling.

This stage incorporated the recognition that when people are angry, worried, and suspicious, they tend to think with the emotional areas of their brains. Throwing a bunch of data and information at them won't work, because the rational areas of their brains are turned off. In fact, it usually only makes them angrier and more worried and suspicious. To win people over, communicators must accept and deal with emotions before they can break through and inform, educate, and persuade with facts.

Covello and Sandman identify the U.S. Environmental Protection Agency's (EPA) "Seven Cardinal Rules of Risk Communication" as a seminal moment in the shift to third-stage application of risk communication principles. The EPA's adoption of these rules was the first time that a government agency acknowledged that experts and the general public perceive and assess risk differently, and that the best way to communicate with people when they're angry, worried, and suspicious is to engage them. Here are the EPA's cardinal rules:

▶ Accept and involve the public as a legitimate partner.
▶ Listen to the audience.
▶ Be honest, frank, and open.
▶ Coordinate and collaborate with other credible sources.
▶ Meet the needs of the media.
▶ Speak clearly and with compassion.
▶ Plan carefully and evaluate performance.

Though originally published almost 25 years ago, these cardinal rules remain relevant in the second decade of the third millennium and will appear again and again throughout this book.

BEYOND TRADITIONAL APPLICATIONS

Over the past quarter century, many government and industry leaders have applied the rules and principles of risk communication in public-health and environmental arenas. That's where policy makers first began to incorporate risk into policy and decision making, as well as where the general public first had the opportunity to assert its power to question and oppose. Certainly my firm applies those rules and principles in those arenas, with the utility trying to build a new power line being a good example.

We've also expanded their application to entirely new arenas, including just about any tough situation in which you may find yourself as a communicator. We've learned that the strategies, skills, and tactics needed to win people over when they're angry, worried, and suspicious of everything you say are necessary and effective not only when you're trying to site a controversial facility or explain an environmental spill or disaster but also in much more common circumstances. Examples that we'll explore include reprimanding or terminating an employee, defending yourself against inaccurate allegations, testifying before a congressional hearing, conducting media interviews, rebranding your company or organization, and sharing information about a chief executive officer's financial impropriety with employees and other audiences.

While the strategies, skills, and techniques involved in breaking through and winning people over are based on sound science, the science itself won't help when you find yourself trying to communicate in a tough situation. What matters most is the proper application of the right strategies, skills, and tactics—in other words, the art that makes the science come alive.

Learning the science is relatively straightforward; mastering the art requires focused practice and application. So let's get started by laying a foundation on which we can begin to build the strategies, skills, and techniques you'll need when the going gets tough and you need to win people over when they're angry, worried, and suspicious of everything you say.

Chapter 2

LAYING THE FOUNDATION

Always turn a negative situation into a positive situation.

—MICHAEL JORDAN
BASKETBALL PLAYER

M any of my firm's clients have been with us for a long time. Our history with one goes back more than 10 years, and virtually from the beginning, this particular organization talked about developing a new name, logo, and tagline. It's a professional membership society, so its mission is to serve that profession by providing certification, education, and networking opportunities. The profession it represents had changed dramatically over time, and the organization's existing brand no longer reflected the reality of its membership. Younger people—emerging professionals—were becoming less likely to join. When we surveyed the membership, the message came through loud and clear: it's time for a change.

Members of professional societies, particularly those who have belonged for many years, often develop very strong attachments and loyalties. They tend to resist change, and because they don't have much experience in the field of communication, they can get bogged down in details and minutiae. It's not a criticism; it's just the reality. Change is hard for just about everyone, especially when it involves something people care about very deeply.

The process of coming up with a new name, logo, and tagline for this group dragged on for months. On several occasions, we thought we had consensus, only to see it evaporate time and time again. Our client was very nervous about how the members would react to a very big change. After a lot of hard work by a lot of dedicated people, my firm presented our proposed branding concept to the group's board of directors at its annual meeting. The directors' response was overwhelmingly positive and very gratifying; they couldn't help but lodge a few minor complaints, of course, but in general, they loved it.

In fact, they loved it so much that they decided to present it to the organization's top 200 leaders at that very meeting— just three days after we presented it to the board. We hadn't expected that, and we didn't have much time to prepare for a gathering that could very well develop into a tough situation. Though the board's uniformly positive reaction to the concept was encouraging, we had no way of knowing how the broader membership would react.

We applied every strategy, skill, and technique for breaking through and winning people over that we had at our disposal. Express care and empathy. Tell stories. Stay positive. Dress appropriately. Send the right nonverbal signals. Cite independent data. Bridge to messages. Avoid traps that can erode trust and credibility. Practice and rehearse. And we did all of this in the course of a few days.

I'm pleased to report that our application of these strategies, skills, and techniques paid off. Though we faced a few hostile questions during the presentation of the new brand concept, and certainly a handful of people left the room unhappy, the situation never got tough. We successfully overcame a big hurdle that allowed us to move forward with implementation of the revitalized brand.

The experience reinforced once again the importance of the fundamental principles upon which the strategies, skills, and techniques associated with breaking through and winning people over are based. In this case, our clients didn't have much time to absorb those principles. They picked them up on the fly and with a lot of our help. Fortunately, we have more time to review those principles in this format. We'll start with four key ideas that it takes to win people over, and then we'll wrap up the chapter with a few words about how jargon interferes when you try to apply those principles.

FOUR EQUATIONS AT THE HEART OF WINNING PEOPLE OVER

To be an effective communicator in tough situations when people are angry, worried, and suspicious of everything you say, it's essential to understand the principles upon which the relevant strategies, skills, and techniques are built. Learning those principles is a useful exercise, too, because as you read through subsequent chapters, you'll be able to trace all of your newfound abilities right back to them.

Let's start with some basic math. Many of the people I train, particularly those with a liberal arts background like my own, recoil at the idea that successful communication requires math. But I assure you that we're talking about arithmetic rather than calculus—just four simple equations that will flow through all of the information presented throughout the rest the book.

Here are the four equations that provide the basic foundation for the strategies, skills, and techniques we're going to discuss:

$P = R$ Perception equals reality.
$E > F$ Emotions trump facts.
$S = B+$ Success comes from being positive.
$3P = HC$ Third parties translate into higher credibility.

If you keep these in mind, everything from here on out will make sense and come together more easily. Also, remember that these apply to any communication situation, whether you're talking to a group, transmitting e-mail, or being interviewed on television (see Figure 2.1).

PERCEPTION EQUALS REALITY

The first equation is the most fundamental:

$$P = R$$

This stands for "Perception equals reality." When communicating with people in tough situations, you are always operating on the P side of this equation. What counts is your audience's *per-*

FIGURE 2.1 The Same Principles Apply, Regardless of the
Form of Communication

While most of the examples I cite in this book involve verbal communication and direct engagement with an audience, the strategies, skills, and
techniques necessary to win people over apply equally in any form of communication. If you have to write a difficult memo to your staff or produce
a fact sheet explaining a problem to concerned citizens near one of your
company's facilities, keep those same strategies, skills, and techniques
in mind. They are especially important if you ever find yourself being
interviewed by the media, whether print, radio, TV, or online. Those can be
among the toughest situations in which you'll ever find yourself. We'll go
into great detail about breaking through and winning people over through
the media in Chapter 8.

©iStockphoto.com/IvanMikhaylov

ception of what is happening (the reason audience members are
angry, worried, and suspicious) and of whether or not you are a
trustworthy and credible source of information. You may understand the reality of the situation: that you don't really represent
any risk to them, that you're really working in their best inter-

ests, that you're telling them the truth, and that they can trust and believe what you are saying. Unfortunately, what you think doesn't matter. Your audience's perception is what matters.

In 2012, my firm worked with a professional society that unfortunately discovered that its long-time executive director had engaged in a series of financial improprieties. Once an internal investigation revealed the extent of the executive director's behavior, the society's board terminated him. The facts were fairly straightforward, and even the executive director did not dispute the investigation's initial findings (though he claimed that what he had done did not rise to the level of a fireable offense). The board chairman drafted and sent a brief e-mail to the group's members, explaining what had happened and why the executive director had been terminated and his membership in the group revoked.

That's when all hell broke loose.

A large number of members recoiled at the news. They knew the executive director, an industry icon with more than 30 years of experience, as an honest and extremely influential leader. Many considered him a friend, and almost everyone thought of him as one of the group's founding fathers. They simply refused to believe he could be guilty of unethical behavior. Their perception of him clashed with the reality of the situation, and the perception prevailed. Suddenly, the group's board and staff found themselves facing a mini-revolt. That's when they called my firm.

We decided that the board chair had to send a second e-mail. It needed to apologize for the tone of the first communication and acknowledge that, while the termination would stand, the board would reevaluate its decision to revoke the executive director's membership once it had completed a full investigation. The message also pledged to keep the members informed of new developments and provided the acting executive director's e-mail address so people could ask questions of him directly.

In other words, we encouraged our client to see the event through the eyes—and perceptions—of its members and act accordingly. Most members perceived the executive director to be an honest, ethical person. The board was telling them their perception was wrong. Because of the way the board had communicated with them, members rejected the facts. Simply stating the facts and failing to address the members' perceptions made the situation worse. The board didn't win anyone over.

I'm pleased to report that the second e-mail was much better received. Many of the members who had been offended by the first communication praised the board and staff for responding to their concerns and so quickly addressing them. The controversy over the executive director's termination essentially disappeared, and the society was able to pivot toward the future and begin the process of finding a new leader.

FACTS DO NOT EQUAL EMOTION

As you read this book, you may find yourself asking, "Why can't I just tell people the facts? Isn't that enough? Why do I need all these fancy techniques this guy is peddling?" When this happens, remember the $P = R$ equation. It helps to explain why a bunch of facts, as true or real as they may be, won't help you win people over. That principle is built into our next equation as well:

$$E > F$$

Or, in tough situations, emotions are greater than—and trump —facts.

When people are angry, worried, and suspicious, they absorb and sift through information with the emotional areas of their brains. The process is chemical, but it helps to think of it as a physical barrier. When the brain's emotional centers are lighting up with thoughts and fears triggered by outside stimuli, facts will not penetrate into the rational part of most people's brains. It's one way to think about "breaking through." If we don't address and calm emotions first, the facts, data, and information we try to communicate will (figuratively) bounce off people's emotions.

Mark Pettinelli, author of *The Psychology of Emotions, Feelings and Thoughts*, summarized this concept nicely:

> Some things in life cause people to feel, these are called emotional reactions. Some things in life cause people to think, these are sometimes called logical or intellectual reactions. Thus life is divided between things that make you feel and things that make you think. The question is, if someone is feeling, does that mean that they are thinking less? It probably does. If part of your brain is being occupied by feeling, then it makes sense that you have less capacity for thought. That is obvious if you

take emotional extremes, such as crying, where people can barely think at all.

Pettinelli argues, and many other researchers agree, that most people have a very difficult time thinking and feeling at the same time. One usually dominates the other. When people are feeling—or, for our purposes, using the emotional portions of their brains—they're looking for an emotional response.

Many of my clients are scientists and engineers, and this equation is one of the hardest for them to digest and accept. They work with facts all day. Facts and data are the currency of their professions, dollars and coins that they trade back and forth. They use facts to convince and persuade, and among colleagues, the best facts (usually) win the day. Yet when they find themselves facing an angry, worried, and suspicious audience and the facts they've relied on throughout their careers have no impact on how that audience thinks or feels—and, in fact, make things worse—they get flustered. That's why some of the smartest people I've met over the course of my career are often the least effective in tough situations.

When people are thinking emotionally, they expect an emotional response. In 1988, Vice President George H. W. Bush and Massachusetts governor Michael Dukakis ran against each other for the presidency. At the time the death penalty was a controversial issue, and the candidates talked about it frequently on the campaign trail. It came up most prominently during their second debate, when CNN anchor Bernard Shaw asked Dukakis, "Governor, if Kitty Dukakis were raped and murdered, would you favor an irrevocable death penalty for the killer?"

Dukakis replied, "No, I don't, and I think you know that I've opposed the death penalty during all of my life."

One of my firm's former employees happened to be in the press room at that debate. As he tells it, the room erupted in a big moan because most of the people there immediately recognized that he had stumbled. At that point in the campaign, Dukakis was already behind in the polls. That one answer, utterly devoid of emotion when emotion was exactly what almost everyone watching wanted and expected to hear from him, put the election out of reach for good. Most of the reporters in the press room concluded that the election was essentially over at that point.

This disconnect between fact and emotion plays out in personal relationships, too (and forms the basis for a lot of stand-up comedy). If you're a man like me, your first instinct when a woman in your life is angry or upset is to try to fix the problem. I don't take you out to dinner often enough? Let's go tonight. You didn't like that necklace I bought for you? I'll return it tomorrow and buy you something nicer. I don't help enough around the house? I'll do the dishes from now on.

The problem is, she's not looking for solutions. She's looking for reassurance and empathy. She wants to know that you understand how she feels. Sure, she'd love more dinners at nice restaurants. Mostly, she's sharing emotions with you because she wants you to validate them. By throwing a bunch of "facts" at her that you believe will solve the problem, you make things worse. When you acknowledge the effect your behavior has on her and on your relationship, and pledge to be more considerate and understanding, you make things better. (You'd think I'd do this more often, but the axiom that those who can't do teach applies a little more than it should in this instance.)

It plays out differently in personal relationships in which both parties are emotionally attached, but the principle is the same. Facts regurgitated in response to emotional concerns almost always backfire.

SUCCESS COMES FROM BEING POSITIVE

The importance of emotions brings us to equation number three:

$$S = B^+$$

This is mathematical shorthand for "To achieve success, you have to be positive." You might be surprised at how seldom this principle is followed. My firm often works with clients facing serious crises. They're often on the defensive, fielding hostile questions from all kinds of angry, worried, and suspicious people: customers, regulators, reporters, etc. In these situations, it's very easy to slip into negative-speak:

"No, we didn't do that!"
"That's not what happened."
"We don't see it that way."
"My company would never do anything like that."

We encourage our clients to be positive, in words and in actions. No matter how tough a situation may be, they have a story to tell—a good story. Too often, they adopt a defensive crouch, both figuratively and literally. They know they're going to be attacked, and they want to protect themselves, like an armadillo rolling itself up into a ball when a predator appears.

The Perils of Negativity

Too often, defensiveness becomes a self-fulfilling prophecy. Act defensive, and that's how you'll come across. People who are angry, worried, and suspicious of everything you say will key off that posture and only become angrier and more worried and suspicious. It's very difficult to be positive from a defensive mind-set, making it all the more difficult to win people over.

Instead, you need to be as positive as possible. You have a story to tell, and you can choose how to tell it. That means sending all the right nonverbal messages (as we'll discuss in Chapter 6). It also means avoiding negative statements and words whenever possible. Research shows that angry, worried, and suspicious people hear and react more intensely to negative words and phrases. This helps to explain why big corporations spend so much time and money protecting and bolstering their brands. If something goes wrong, they know that all the negative publicity they receive will quickly overwhelm anything positive that has come before. So when they are not in the middle of a crisis, they relentlessly convey positive messages about themselves to consumers, regulators, and others. The goal is to drive positive feelings so high that even a torrent of more powerful negative messages won't sway people against them permanently. This also can help them recover more quickly.

In tough situations, the context of negative words and phrases doesn't really matter. At the height of the Watergate scandal, Richard Nixon uttered the now-infamous assertion "People have got to know whether or not their president's a crook. Well, I'm not a crook." The sentiment only served to drive his approval ratings lower. His use of a negative phrase, "not a crook," to defend himself made things worse. Rather than hearing the whole sentence, most people simply heard "crook" and thought even less of the president because he was being negative. Not that it necessarily would have helped him much, but Nixon would have been much better off saying something like this: "People have got to know whether or not their president obeys the law. Well, I do obey the law."

Use positive words as often as possible in tough situations. In Chapter 10, we're going to discuss the difference between "credibility questions" and "fact questions." It's especially important to avoid negative words when answering credibility questions, because they strike at the heart of your trustworthiness and credibility. When responding to more straightforward fact questions, negative words are more acceptable. But in either case, positive words are always better.

Avoiding negative words can be difficult. When people accuse you of lying to them or harming their families or ruining their lives in a tough situation, chances are, you're going to want to reply, "No, I'm not doing that." But it's much more effective to say, "I'm here to tell you the truth," or "Your family is perfectly safe," or "I'm trying to make things better."

I'm writing this book in the midst of the 2012 presidential campaign. Millions of Americans are being bombarded by negative ads from the candidates and their political parties. Now you know part of the reason why. Negatives are powerful, and to the extent that the electorate is angry, worried, and suspicious (and they are), negative messages overwhelm positive messages—at least in the minds of voters who haven't already decided for whom to vote.

Another good reason to squeeze negative words from your vocabulary is that using them almost always leads you to repeat whatever allegation someone is levying against you:

Audience member: Why are you lying to me?
You: I'm not lying to you.

Or:

Audience member: The pollution from your factory is making me sick.
You: The pollution from my factory is not making you sick.

Or:

Reporter: How many of your products are tainted with salmonella?
You: None of my products are tainted with salmonella.

THIRD PARTIES TRANSLATE INTO HIGHER CREDIBILITY

Our fourth and final equation is this:

$$3P = HC$$

In this book, we're going to talk about credibility over and over again. Along with trust, credibility is absolutely essential for breaking through and winning people over. One way to boost your credibility is to borrow a little of it from someone who has more than you do. In my business, we call these people third parties, so this equation stands for "Third parties translate into higher credibility."

This was certainly true when my firm worked with the utility I mentioned in Chapter 1. As you can imagine, the decision to build a new high-voltage transmission line created a lot of controversy in the communities where the line was supposed to run. People worried about noise, electric and magnetic fields (EMF), aesthetics, property values, and many other issues. As a big, faceless corporation perceived to be concerned with nothing more than the bottom line, the utility didn't have much trustworthiness or credibility in the eyes of local residents.

Among many other recommendations, we encouraged the utility to cite independent studies when talking about the line. These included studies by the following sources:

▶ Government agencies, which could show that the power line was necessary to ensure a steady flow of reliable electricity for the region
▶ Academics knowledgeable about the nature of EMF, who could describe their very limited impact, if any, on health
▶ Real estate experts, who could show that power lines do not reduce property values where they're built

We didn't want the utility telling people these things. We wanted government officials, academics, and other experts to tell them, because those groups have much more credibility with people than corporate representatives.

And to keep the promise that I made in Chapter 1, here's what happened: The new line is on hold, but not because of community opposition. With our help, the utility was very successful in winning people over. But in the meantime, the Great Recession reduced projected demand for electricity to the point that regulators decided the line wasn't needed, at least for the foreseeable future.

On most studies related to trust and credibility, corporate representatives wind up near the bottom of the scale. Who are the most credible sources? Independent scientists and engineers tend to have a lot of credibility with people generally, as do academics, teachers, and doctors. Government officials can be good sources from which to borrow credibility, but it really depends on the specific person, office, and agency. The U.S. Centers for Disease Control and Prevention has tremendous credibility with the general public, for example, but the U.S. Department of Energy has very little.

When you are seeking to take advantage of third-party credibility, keep the following points in mind.

Make Sure People You Borrow from Have More Credibility than You

Credibility works both ways. If you cite a source with less credibility than you, your credibility will go down. Lawyers generally are held in very low esteem, for example, as are public relations professionals (but don't hold that against me). People who work for government agencies as career employees tend to have higher credibility than people who are appointed or elected, though many politicians are very credible. Studies consistently show that Americans like and trust their own member of Congress, for example, but not the other 434 members of the House of Representatives.

Relative Credibility Can Change

Just because a third party is credible today doesn't mean he or she will be tomorrow, and vice versa. Credibility rises and falls (see Figure 2.2). Since I picked on him earlier, I'll use Richard Nixon as an example again. He resigned in disgrace, but by the time he died 20 years later, most people saw him as a very credible expert on foreign policy. Tiger Woods once had a lot of credibility, but not so much anymore. If he wins a few more major golf tournaments and stays out of the gossip columns, that will change with time. NASA, typically one of the most credible government agencies, suffered a big drop in credibility after the space shuttle *Challenger* exploded during launch in 1986 and again when the *Columbia* broke apart coming home in 2003. As I'm writing this, the agency's Curiosity rover just landed safely on Mars, so NASA's credibility is on the upswing.

In deciding whom to cite as a credible source in order to bolster your own credibility, pay attention to the news surrounding different sources. Say you've cited an engineer from the local university in the past. Suddenly, the university's president is fired for embezzling funds. Now that engineer is off limits for a while. Even if she had absolutely nothing to do with the scandal, her credibility is tainted by the diminished credibility of the organization for which she worked. Wait until you're sure that

FIGURE 2.2 Relative Credibility Is Ever Changing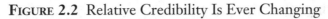

Since credibility transference works both ways, you have to be careful to cite sources that will add to your credibility rather than detract from it. Relative levels of credibility change all the time. When I first started helping people communicate in tough situations, my list of credible sources always included clergy along with scientists and doctors. Not anymore. Given the scandals involving child molestation and the Roman Catholic Church, I now urge people not to borrow credibility from religious leaders, all of whom unfortunately get painted with the same brush, at least as far as credibility goes. This will change again in time. As the church acknowledges its past and institutes reforms, eventually the scandal will fade, and priests (and other clergy) will regain some of the credibility they've lost.

©iStockphoto.com/small_frog

citing that engineer won't evoke negative thoughts and images in the minds of your audience members. In the wake of a scandal like this one, I'd wait at least six months and ideally one year.

Even as you pay attention to what's in the news, keep in mind that most of us don't trust the media. The Gallup organization has been monitoring the public's confidence in the media for decades. In a September 2012 press release, Gallup announced that America's trust in media fell to an all-time low. Only 40 percent of Americans indicated that they had a "great deal" or a "fair amount" of confidence in the media. The drop-off in media credibility has been even more dramatic over earlier years, as it has been for many other institutions. In the 1970s, confidence in the media ran as high as 72 percent. Today, citing the media can be a dicey proposition, even as the media can have a big impact on the credibility of the people in their stories.

The Closer a Source to Your Target Audience, the Greater Its Credibility

Studies routinely find that people place the highest level of trust and credibility in people "like them" or people they know—neighbors, friends, and peers. In April 2012, the Nielsen Company released its annual Global Trust in Advertising survey. When 28,000 Internet respondents in 56 countries were asked, "To what extent do you trust the following sources of advertising?" the overwhelming number one answer was, "Recommendations from people I know." More than nine in ten respondents said they completely or somewhat trust what amounts to word-of-mouth advertising. The number two answer, cited by seven out of ten respondents, was, "Consumer opinions posted online." No other form of advertising broke 50 percent.

The bias favoring people like us or people we know translates to geography as well. A professor at a local university typically will be more credible than one who works far away, even at a top school like Harvard or Princeton. A local public official—say, the town mayor—will be more credible than a representative from the state government or Washington, D.C., all other things being equal. You can even play this game internationally. Studies by British academics carry more weight with most Americans than studies by almost any other foreign nationality, largely because of the "special relationship" between the two countries. After the United States invaded Iraq in 2003, France came under a lot of criticism for refusing to join the coalition forces. This was the era of "freedom fries." For several years afterward, we warned clients not to cite French sources in an attempt to gain credibility. However, that's no longer true today.

JUNK THE JARGON

Every industry and profession comes loaded with jargon. We throw it around without giving it a second thought. My own business, public relations, is no different. Hits, metrics, earned media, PRSA, infographics—when I use these terms in talking to my colleagues and clients, they understand. When I use them with friends and family, they usually have no idea what I'm talking about. Not that it bothers them. If they're really interested, they'll ask. Otherwise, they just let the jargon go by and don't hold it against me.

In tough situations, however, the normal rules of communication do not apply. Everything you do and say, including jargon, is perceived through the most negative filter possible. Jargon confuses and muddles your message. Even worse, when people are angry, worried, and suspicious, they perceive jargon to be condescending. They think you're trying to show them how much smarter you are than they are, as if you're saying, "If only you knew as much about this topic as I do, you would understand." Finally, jargon tends to involve a lot of facts and data, which violates equation number two.

When communicating in tough situations, you have to strike a careful balance between talking over people's heads and talking down to them. The standard you should shoot for is *USA Today*. While you'll get slightly different answers from different experts, the general consensus is that *USA Today* is written for people with an eighth- or ninth-grade education. Stories are made up of short sentences and use simple words rarely longer than three syllables. When you find yourself in a tough situation and need to win people over, think about how you would talk to the average 14- or 15-year-old. Would you include a lot of complicated jargon in a conversation with an eighth-grader? Probably not. (By way of comparison, experts generally consider the *New York Times* to be aimed at people with a tenth- or eleventh-grade education.)

This isn't necessarily a criticism of the American educational system. People who are angry, worried, and suspicious process information through a different filter. They're thinking with the emotional rather than the rational portions of their brains. Even the smartest people may have more trouble than usual hearing and understanding when their emotions are in control.

If you absolutely must use jargon, make sure to explain it. In my business, for example, a "hit" means a media placement—a story we helped get published in a newspaper or aired on television. This rule applies when someone else uses jargon, too. If you're speaking to a group of people and someone asks you a question that includes jargon, explain it before you respond. My firm has run across trained activists at public meetings who deliberately ask questions containing a lot of jargon. They hope that, by getting you to repeat it, they'll drive down your trust and credibility.

Scrubbing jargon from your vocabulary can be harder than it sounds, because much of it goes beyond the more obvious technical words and phrases. Even general business terms that you may throw around at work every day—say, fiscal year, third-quarter earnings, and COB (close of business)—can be jargon to others. People who don't work in an office environment won't understand even this seemingly simple and innocent jargon.

By now I'm sure you have a sense that this book is really about trust and credibility. We'll return to that topic in Chapter 5. First, in Chapter 3, we're going to look at the vital role that storytelling plays in winning people over and then, in Chapter 4, at what drives people to become angry, worried, and suspicious of everything you say in the first place, making trust and credibility qualities all-important. We'll see that learning how people perceive and assess risk and come to accept it (or not) is essential to understanding why we find ourselves in tough situations that make it so much more difficult to break through and win people over.

Chapter 3

The Lost Art of Storytelling

To hell with facts! We need stories!

—Ken Kesey, novelist

In the public relations business, we spend a lot of time talking about, developing, honing, and conveying messages (sometimes known as sound bites). They are the words and ideas we want our clients' audiences to remember, the ones that will resonate and (hopefully) inspire them to change their attitudes, beliefs, and actions.

We typically talk about messages in terms of a triangle, which is nothing more than a device for developing three messages and then building upon them to create a full-fledged messaging platform. While it's unclear who invented the message triangle, my firm credits communications consultant Michael Sheehan. Sheehan helped to develop Bill Clinton's message triangle during his successful run for the presidency in 1992. It looked like the one shown in Figure 3.1, and candidate Clinton was relentless in driving it home during that campaign. (By the way, this message triangle may look familiar. Barack Obama used a very similar one on his way to the White House in 2008.)

FIGURE 3.1 Bill Clinton's Message Triangle

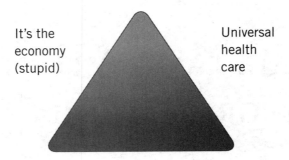

It's the
economy
(stupid)

Universal
health
care

Change (Democrats) v. more
of the same (Republicans)

When he ran for president in 1992, Bill Clinton was relentless about conveying the three messages depicted in this message triangle. No matter where he was or what he was doing—participating in a debate, appearing in a campaign ad, or hosting a town hall meeting—Clinton always talked about universal health care, the need to focus on getting the economy going again, and the need to change party control of the White House after 12 years of Republican rule. *Barbara Longsworth*

The device is a triangle, not a square or a pentagon, because research shows that most people can hold no more than three independent thoughts in their minds before the information begins to muddle together and becomes overwhelming. It's the law of diminishing marginal returns: at some point, too much information confuses more than it clarifies. Research also shows that this point comes much sooner when people are angry, worried, and suspicious.

Messages are important; in Chapter 10, we'll talk about the role they play in my firm's model for answering difficult questions in tough situations. But after more than 20 years in the PR business, I've come to the conclusion that my profession puts a little too much emphasis on locking into the repetition of messages and sound bites. You can see the effect every weekend on the Sunday-morning talk shows: politicians and political consultants have become so relentlessly focused on conveying messages or talking points that they rarely, if ever, actually answer a question. They've become robotic and predictable. I know exactly what someone representing Democrats and someone representing Republicans is going to say. So I tune out.

The phenomenon has filtered into the business world as well. CEOs and other corporate spokespeople often use the same messages endlessly to defend their companies. The messages may be well researched and true, but the way they're used has become cliché. No matter what the question, the respondent always bridges to a message (more on the art of bridging in Chapter 8). However, the response should come more often in the form of a relatable story. In some cases, the answer only needs to be yes or no—particularly in response to one of those "fact questions" we touched on in Chapter 2.

I've pounded home the preeminence of staying on message hundreds of times myself. I freely admit I'm part of the problem, but with this book, I hope to make you part of the solution. Rather than focusing exclusively on repeating messages, people who hope to convince an angry, worried, and suspicious audience—whether one person or many—should embed their messages and other important information within compelling stories as well as within genuine answers to questions. In tough situations, when facts and data rarely penetrate because people are thinking with the emotional portions of their brains, stories get through.

THE POWER OF A STORY

In an August 2012 *New York Times Magazine* article about storytelling and changing minds, author Maggie Koerth-Baker makes the point succinctly:

> People change their minds all the time, even about very important matters. It's just hard to do when the stakes are high. That's why marshaling data and making rational arguments won't work. Whether you're changing your own mind or someone else's, the key is emotional, persuasive storytelling.

To illustrate the point, let me tell a story of my own.

David Axelrod, one of President Obama's senior political advisers, is a frequent guest on the Sunday-morning talk shows. It's clear that before each appearance, he huddles with a couple of Democratic Party operatives to review the messages of the day. When the camera's red light comes on, no matter what the interviewer asks him, he repeats those messages one after the other after the other.

I'm sure that's what he was trained to do—and trained well. No doubt Axelrod is a message master. But after seeing him a few times, I got tired of him constantly spouting the party line. First I disliked him, and then I simply stopped listening to him. (I'm picking on Axelrod, for reasons that will become apparent later in the chapter, but many of his Republican and Democratic colleagues are just as guilty of engaging in "message-speak.")

I continued to feel this way until one Sunday in the midst of the 2012 presidential campaign when Axelrod appeared on ABC's *This Week*. I had the show on in the background while I was doing the dishes. I knew the topic was health care, but I was adhering to my no-Axelrod policy and not paying attention. Then something he said caught my ear (I'm paraphrasing here):

> My daughter Lauren has suffered from epilepsy her whole life. So my family and I know all too well the stress that comes from caring for a loved one and not knowing what we were going to do when our health insurance ran out. Thankfully, Lauren is doing well now, but I remember those dark early days when we worried almost as much about reaching the lifetime cap on our insurance policy as we did about her . . .

Suddenly he had me hanging on his every word. After telling the story about his daughter, Axelrod went on to explain how the Affordable Care Act removed the lifetime cap on insurance payouts. Never again would families have to worry about running out of insurance, as he and his wife had worried many years ago.

He conveyed a message, but he made it orders of magnitude more powerful by telling a story rather than parroting a sound bite. Not only did I learn something (I had had no idea the health care law passed in 2010 removed the lifetime cap on insurance payments, nor had I known he had a daughter with epilepsy), but Axelrod also accomplished something I never thought he could. He turned me into a fan. That one anecdote, told simply and concisely, completely changed my mind about him. He became more human, and once he did, I was more interested in what he had to say. I liked him, so I was more willing to listen to him. It also happened to make me a little more supportive of President Obama's health care law, which of course had been Axelrod's goal all along. He accomplished it not with facts or messages or sound bites, but with a story.

Why? Because his story resonated with me as a parent. I have two teenagers, a son and a daughter. Thankfully, they've always been healthy. Unlike millions of Americans, I've never had to worry about a lifetime cap or, even worse, going without insurance at all. But after listening to Axelrod, I could sure understand what that must feel like. Because of that story, I related to Axelrod in a way I never had before. He broke through and won me over. That's the power of storytelling, and it's a lost art that you need to revive in order to become an effective communicator in tough situations.

TIPS ON HOW TO TELL COMPELLING STORIES

Storytelling, like any other art form, is a skill. Some people have a natural affinity for it. Franklin Roosevelt, Ronald Reagan, and Martin Luther King Jr. are just a few well-known examples, though even they put in a lot of hard work to hone their natural skills (see Figure 3.2 for an example). Fortunately, you don't have to rise to their level to succeed—though that's a great goal to set for yourself!

While my firm continues to spend time developing and perfecting messages and helping our clients convey them with

FIGURE 3.2 Even Natural Storytellers Need Practice

Some people are natural storytellers, but even they had to hone their natural-born abilities before they became great communicators. Ronald Reagan was not a particularly compelling storyteller before he took a job as a pitchman for General Electric. He traveled the country for years, speaking to different groups and promoting GE products. Over time, long before he became a politician, he learned how to connect with an audience and tell stories to which they could relate. It served him very well when he first ran for governor of California in 1966, and it continued to pay dividends right through the end of his presidency. One of President Reagan's greatest stories, told in West Berlin near the end of his second term, contained perhaps his most-remembered line: "Mr. Gorbachev, Mr. Gorbachev, tear down this wall." I still get chills when I hear it. In fact, I just got chills as I wrote it.

impact, we now spend just as much time working with clients to sharpen their storytelling skills. If you do an Internet search for "tips on how to be a good storyteller," you'll find enough information to fill a thousand books. While you're welcome to do so, I'll try to save you a little time by sharing the basic storytelling rules that my firm emphasizes with our clients.

Be Ready

If part of your job is to communicate, especially in tough situations, you must have stories to tell. We'll spend more time on how to get some stories in the next chapter, but let me give you an example here.

One of my partners was fired early in his career. On the few occasions when we've had to let someone go from my firm (a situation where we're very definitely dealing with someone who may be angry, worried, and suspicious—often all three), we let my partner take the lead. He happens to be a very empathetic and comforting person, but even more than that, he can relate the story of when he lost a job. That immediately resonates with the employee, which always makes a very difficult conversation much easier for everyone involved.

Be Relevant

Telling any old story won't do. It has to be a relatable story, and one that your audience finds credible. David Axelrod's story worked because it was relevant to the topic at hand. Not all stories are gems. During his one debate with Republican candidate Ronald Reagan, Jimmy Carter responded to a question about nuclear weapons by referring to a conversation he had had the day before with his daughter, Amy. He told the brief story because she answered "nuclear proliferation" when he asked what issue she thought was most important. It fell flat; indeed, he came under a lot of (perhaps unfair) criticism for supposedly basing his policies on his then 12-year-old daughter's opinions.

Business executives often make the same mistake. Tony Hayward, former chief executive officer of BP, did so in the wake of his company's Gulf of Mexico oil spill in April 2010. In his response to a reporter's question about the impact of the spill on the people who lived along the Gulf Coast, he said, "We're sorry for the massive disruption it's caused to their lives. There's no one who wants this thing over more than I do. I'd like my life back."

While it wasn't much of a story, it was clearly an attempt to empathize with and relate to average people—one that failed miserably. Tony Hayward is a very wealthy man. The life he wanted back included a mansion, a yacht, and a private plane. Whatever happened in the gulf, however long it took to clean up the spill, he was going to be fine. Thousands of shrimpers, boatmen, and other people along the Gulf Coast were not going to get their lives back for years. Many were ruined forever.

The people with whom Hayward was trying to connect couldn't relate to his story at all. Less than two months after he uttered that statement, he left BP in disgrace.

Be Brief

Though stories penetrate much more successfully than facts and data in tough situations, the rule about the amount of information people can process still applies. Less is more. Keep your stories short and to the point. The shorter the story, the less chance you'll go off on confusing and unnecessary tangents and lose people in the process. David Axelrod told his story in less than a minute. We encourage our clients to cultivate stories that last no more than two minutes, for reasons that will become clear later in the book. If your stories are running longer than two minutes, you're breaking this rule.

Be Simple

Again and again, we'll come back to the importance of keeping your story simple. In tough situations, the people with whom you're communicating rarely know as much as you do. It's your job to find a way to break through and win them over with simple stories (as well as messages and, ultimately, facts). Trying to convey complicated information by using a lot of technical jargon won't work; instead, it will make things worse.

Simplicity is a key part of relevancy. You want to tell stories that resonate with the greatest number of people, so the way to go is to use simple concepts conveyed in simple words. Axelrod didn't go into great detail about the nature of his daughter's condition or the fine print of his insurance policy. Nor did he try to explain the intricacies of the ultracomplicated Affordable Care Act. My daughter was sick. Our health insurance almost ran out. Thanks to the new health care law, no one will ever have to worry about that again. Perfect.

Be Honest

The importance of honesty may seem obvious, but it's worth mentioning. In Chapter 2, we discussed the $S = B+$ equation. It can be easy to go too far in an attempt to emphasize the positive, especially when we're trying to win over people when they're angry, worried, and suspicious of everything we say. We're all inclined to cover up or downplay bad news, or at least to put the best spin on it that we can. That's a mistake, particularly in a tough situation.

When it comes to telling stories, you might feel compelled to embellish a little, especially if you're under attack. Don't. In a tough situation, your audience will assume you're not being truthful. They'll be looking for any sign, whether verbal or non-verbal, that you're exaggerating, fudging, or outright lying. If you are, they'll know it. Think of dishonesty as a trap. Once you fall in, you won't be able to climb out. In contrast, as the example in Figure 3.3 illustrates, a straightforward approach is refreshing.

FIGURE 3.3 Honesty Is the Best Storytelling Policy

Several years ago, a client called us in to help with the sale of two big manufacturing plants that were close to 50 years old and fairly expensive to operate. At the price being offered, they still represented a bargain, because they faced no competition in their market. The company CEO wanted to avoid talking about the plants' age and expense and instead to focus on the positive. We told him we saw it another way: be honest and address the negatives right at the start. We counseled him to begin his presentation to potential investors this way: "I'm here to sell you two five-decade-old factories that need a lot of maintenance and are expensive to operate. Why would anyone want to buy them? For one reason: to make a lot of money." He jumped at the idea, and the plants sold quickly, for the price he wanted.

And what's wrong with being honest? People—even those who are angry, worried, and suspicious—are generally pretty forgiving creatures. We're all human. We all make mistakes. We all say dumb things from time to time. If you acknowledge a mistake, most people will give you the benefit of the doubt, even in a tough situation. I opened this book with President Clinton's lie about his sexual affair with Monica Lewinsky. What would have happened had he simply owned up to the mistake and apologized for it? He would have taken hell, for sure. Would he have been impeached? I doubt it. After all, he wasn't impeached for having an affair. The charges against him involved perjury and obstruction of justice—in other words, lying.

How about Tony Hayward? What if he had said something along these lines?

> We obviously made a big mistake here. Something went horribly wrong, and we're going to do whatever it takes to figure out what happened, clean up the mess, and make sure it never happens again. And I'm not going home until that is done and the people who were affected by the spill get their lives back.

I bet he'd still have his job.

One last example that many more of us will face in our lives: Several times, I've referred to letting an employee go as a classic tough situation. In some cases, perhaps the fault lies with you, rather than the employee. Maybe you hired someone without the right skills for the job. If so, say so. Disarming candor is a great way to win people over.

Avoid PowerPoint

I once read an article that described PowerPoint as "technological cocaine." If that's true, it's time to break the addiction. My firm counsels against using it (or any similar program) in most situations, and forbids it for clients heading into tough situations. In Chapter 5, I'm going to introduce you to a client I'll call Mr. Malone. Here's a little preview: Mr. Malone needed help preparing for a very difficult meeting with an auditorium full of outraged citizens. When we first met, he shared the PowerPoint he intended to present. It included dozens and dozens of complicated slides. Our first recommendation: chuck the whole thing. Don't overwhelm people with data and facts and charts. Just talk to them, one human being to another. And tell a story. We'll see how that worked out for him.

My partners and I have seen it many times. We're sitting in a conference hall watching speaker after speaker run through their PowerPoint bullets and data. Meanwhile, everyone around us is reading the newspaper or thumbing through their smartphones or dozing off. Then a new speaker steps up to the podium and says, "Let me tell you a story," and every head in the room jerks up to listen.

I encourage you to avoid PowerPoint for several reasons:

▶ *The very programming itself is anti-story.* With PowerPoint, there's no beginning, middle, or end—just a bunch of statements with supporting data in no particular order. Sure, most presenters include an "introduction" slide and a "conclusions" slide, but those do not a story make. Stories have arcs. They start off by introducing characters and defining the challenge those characters face. They chronicle the journey that the characters must take to face the challenge. And they conclude with lessons in the form of what the characters learned along their journey and how they have grown.

▶ *It's very hard to do it well.* Done right, PowerPoint presentations can add to a story arc. The right word or photo can enhance the power of the story. In more than 15 years of watching hundreds and hundreds of PowerPoint presentations, I've seen that happen once or twice. All the others, including too many of my own, detracted from the story by incorporating too many words or too many features and by destroying the story arc. On numerous occasions, I've actually watched as presenters simply read the words on their slides one after the other, as if they were giving a speech. Better that they had. In the end, the best and safest way to use PowerPoint is not to use it at all.

▶ *It puts the focus on the screen and the slides, rather than on you.* Communicating in a tough situation is all about establishing trust and credibility by connecting with people in a human way. That's very hard to do when your audience is staring at a screen rather than listening to—and watching—you. Not only are the audience members not watching you, but you're also not watching them. Chances are you're turned away from them to look at the screen or looking down to read off your computer or a prompter. Two of the most important nonverbal signals that you send in tough situations are eye contact and posture. To paraphrase Edward Tufte, perhaps the nation's leading expert on the graphic depiction of information, PowerPoint corrupts trust and credibility. It also contributes to the problem of information overload. Researchers in Australia and elsewhere have found that most people absorb information if it's delivered orally *or* in written form. Doing both at the same time makes it almost impossible to absorb either.

▶ *Too often the technology fails.* It's almost inevitable. Your computer crashes or runs out of power right in the middle of a presentation. Or one of the features you incorporated to make the words slide across the screen doesn't work. It's also common to lower the lights so people can better see the screen. You might as well hand people a pillow.

I'm picking on PowerPoint because it's by far the most well-known and widely used presentation software on the market. Ultimately, any software is going to bring the same disadvantages, so the best approach is to avoid them all.

Ultimately, PowerPoint and other presentation software like it represent crutches that communicators rely on far too much. The software becomes an excuse not to be fully prepared, and when you're trying to break through and win over people when they're angry, worried, and suspicious of everything you say, not being fully prepared is a recipe for disaster.

Keep these tips in mind as we move forward, because the ability to tell a good story will become very important when we discuss the criteria by which people judge whether you're a trustworthy and credible person.

Chapter 4

Real Risk vs. Perceived Risk, or Why We Drive

The risks that kill people and the risks that upset people are completely different.

—Peter Sandman,
RISK COMMUNICATION EXPERT

In October 2002, a sniper terrorized the Washington, D.C., area for three frightening weeks. The sniper (and, as it turned out, his teenage accomplice) shot 13 people. Ten died, and three others survived critical wounds.

I lived in Washington at the time, as I still do. The attacks changed the behavior of almost everyone who lived in the area. I personally witnessed a family sprint from the entrance of a mall to their car, serpentining the whole way in an attempt to offer a less-promising target. Four of the shootings took place at gas stations, so many people, myself included, spent as little time as possible outside their cars while pumping gas. I'd jump out the door, crouch down below the car as I swiped my credit card, jam the nozzle into the tank, and jump back into the car while the tank filled up.

Once the perpetrators were caught and the Washington metropolitan region returned to normal, researchers began to study the public's behavior during the attacks. How did people react to the shootings? Did they change their routines? How so? How did information, or misinformation, affect their assessment of the danger posed by the snipers and therefore their behavior? Was their behavior rational or irrational? Did their actions reduce their risk of being shot? Or did they actually increase their chances of being harmed?

What they discovered intrigued me and helped to solidify my understanding of the issue of risk perception and assessment. Whole books have been written about the topic, but for our purposes, the conclusions drawn by a team of British researchers at the Centre of Risk for Health Care Research and Practice in London are most relevant: Many people, because they did not possess accurate information about the true level of the threat posed by the snipers, changed their behavior in ways that actually put them in greater danger of being harmed in other ways.

Some Washingtonians, particularly among those who lived near gas stations where several of the shootings took place, feared that the snipers would strike twice at the same location. So they drove to more distant gas stations—sometimes as far as 10 or 20 miles away. Because they spent more time on the road, they raised their risk of being injured or killed in an automobile accident. The snipers never returned to the same place twice, so these people's real risk of being shot at their local gas stations was zero. Even if the snipers had returned, the chances that any single person would wind up in the wrong place at the wrong time were not much higher. Pedestrians who were busy looking around for signs of the sniper rather than paying attention to traffic raised their risk of being struck by a car. The family I saw sprinting and serpentining through the mall parking lot was much more likely to be hit by a car backing out of a space than to be shot by the snipers. Walking slowly in a straight line, as a family would have done under normal circumstances, would have been much safer.

Roughly five million people lived in the Washington, D.C., metropolitan area when the shootings took place. The British researchers found that the chances of being shot and killed by the snipers had they been on the loose *for an entire year* would have been 1 in 53,325. As a Washingtonian, I was more than twice as likely to be killed in a car accident, an accidental fall, an accidental poisoning, or a random, run-of-the-mill murder. I remember jumping in and out of my car to avoid the incredibly small risk of being shot. I don't recall strapping myself into the shower to avoid a much more likely fatal slip in my bathtub.

The strategies, skills, and techniques needed to break through and win people over in tough situations are rooted in an ever-evolving understanding of risk assessment and acceptance. Everything we're going to discuss from this point on is designed essentially to help you convince your audience to accept a risk. So a quick primer on the basics of risk—what it means, how we assess it, how we decide whether or not to accept it, why we fear some risks more than others, and how all of this translates into how we perceive risk—is an essential first step. (For those who would like to delve deeper into the fascinating world of risk assessment and perception, the Recommended Reading list at the end of this book lists a number of sources on the subject.)

WHAT WE FEAR DIFFERS FROM WHAT IS DANGEROUS

We usually think about risk in terms of a physical threat: being shot by snipers or hit by a car or succumbing to disease. Less obvious but equally relevant to communicating in tough situations are risks that come in the form of emotional burdens. What if you learned tomorrow that a company wanted to build a landfill less than a mile from your home? While the facility wouldn't threaten your life or the lives of anyone you care about, chances are you'd feel a risk born of emotional burden. You might think you wouldn't be able to enjoy your backyard anymore because the facility would be noisy and smelly. You might worry that the facility would bring a lot more truck traffic to your neighborhood's already-congested streets. You might be concerned that your property would lose value.

Or say your boss tells you he needs to talk to you about a problem at work. You know he isn't going to hit you, so you're not going to worry about your physical safety. But the prospect of a conversation like that creates anxiety and stress—in other words, an emotional burden. When you walk into his office, you're going to be worried for sure, and perhaps even angry and suspicious.

The risk doesn't necessarily need to be aimed directly at you. The poor economy we've suffered through over the past several years imposes emotional burdens on millions of Americans, even those who haven't lost their jobs. Simply the prospect of losing your job, or of someone close to you losing a job, is enough to create an emotional burden that becomes an imposed risk. As a result, our political leaders have been communicating in tough situations the entire time, because the economic anxiety a lot of people feel makes them angry, worried, and suspicious of everything politicians say.

All of these risks, both physical and emotional, change the nature of communication. If a company hopes to build that landfill, your boss wants to make sure you accept what he has to say and that you fix what's wrong, and the president wants to be reelected, they have to find a way to convince you to accept the risk they're imposing on you. Risk creates unique barriers to effective communication that do not exist in our normal, everyday interactions with people. We need to establish trust and credibility in order to break through those barriers and win people over.

As it turns out, human beings today are terrible risk assessors. That wasn't always the case. Thousands of years ago, when our ancestors survived as hunters and gatherers, our risk assessment skills were finely honed. Run from the lion. Don't eat those berries. Somewhere along the way, as we became more civilized and comfortable, our risk assessment skills atrophied. Some behavioral scientists theorize that our brains remain hardwired to fear and avoid risk but haven't adapted to a society that's far more complicated than those that existed not all that long ago. Others speculate that our senses are dulled because we've succeeded in making everyday living so safe and secure.

To paraphrase Peter Sandman, one of the world's foremost experts on communicating about risk, this lack of risk assessment skills leads most of us to fear relatively harmless behaviors and disregard far more dangerous ones. To illustrate the discrepancy between "real risk" and "perceived risk," it helps to think in terms of how dangerous something is to you (toxicity) and how much of it you're likely to come into contact with (exposure). How we perceive the interaction between these two factors often leads to inaccurate assessment of what really poses a risk and what doesn't, as illustrated in Figure 4.1.

Consider plutonium. The bad news is that plutonium, particularly if you inhale it, is extremely toxic—lethal, in fact, even in tiny doses. The good news is that very few of us will ever be exposed to plutonium. Now consider rat poison. It's also very toxic if ingested. Unlike plutonium, rat poison is in plenty of people's cupboards. If you ask a toxicologist which substance presents a bigger risk, she'll tell you it's the rat poison, because the chances of exposure are much higher.

But what scares you more, plutonium or rat poison? My guess is most people would say plutonium, even though rat poison represents the bigger risk. Bruce Schneier, an expert in security risk, has used other examples to illustrate the point: anthrax versus the flu, terrorism versus street crime, flying versus driving. Which scares you more? Probably the first risk in each pair. Which is more dangerous? Most definitely the latter.

Peter Sandman invented an elegant but powerful equation that helps to explain the difference between real risk and perceived risk:

$$Risk = Hazard + Outrage$$

FIGURE 4.1 What Scares Us Isn't Always What Threatens Us

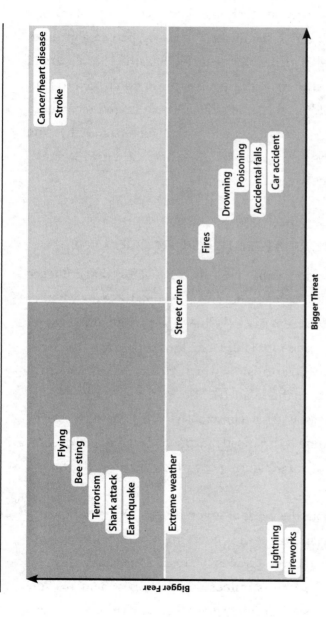

Toxicologists define risk as a function of toxicity (how dangerous something is) and exposure (how likely people are to be exposed). People are notoriously poor risk assessors, as this scatterplot shows. Which of these substances or activities do you worry about most? Many probably lie in the left quadrants, which contains the least-risky examples. Which *should* you worry about most? The ones that lie in the right quadrants. Understanding the difference is critical for communicators who want to win people over.

Barbara Longsworth

Sandman essentially substitutes "hazard" for toxicity, or how dangerous something is. He uses "outrage" as a broader variable for exposure, one that takes into account the many different ways that a risk can anger and worry people and make them suspicious. If risk simply equaled hazard, I would argue that I didn't need to write this book and you don't need to read it. No one would need special strategies, skills, and techniques to communicate, because people would understand the true nature of different risks and would not become angry, worried, and suspicious nearly as often.

MANY FACTORS AFFECT RISK ACCEPTANCE

Outrage is a function of the many different factors that influence risk acceptance. People use dozens of factors to assess whether they're willing to accept a risk. While experts generally agree on which ones have the most influence for the average American citizen, it's impossible to know which factors will affect which people the most or the least. It's also important to remember that few people assess risks consciously. They don't necessarily know they're doing it. It's mostly instinctual, and effective communicators are adept at figuring out which factors are at play in any given situation.

Drawing from the work of noted experts Dr. Paul Slovic, a professor of psychology at the University of Oregon, and David Ropeik and Dr. George Gray at Harvard University, this section describes the factors influencing risk assessment that my firm believes to be most important when you're trying to win people over.

Trust

Of all the factors that influence the acceptance of risk, the most powerful is trust. If we trust the source of a risk we feel is being imposed on us, we're much more likely to accept the risk. Some research suggests that we're *2,000 times* more likely to accept a risk if it comes from someone, or something, we trust. The classic example is driving. According to the National Highway Traffic Safety Administration, more than 32,000 Americans died in motor-vehicle-related accidents in 2011. The lifetime risk of dying in a car accident in the United States is about 1 in 75. We've all known people who lost their lives this way. I'll never forget my high school classmate who lost her life in an accident within view of our school. Or my dad's boss, who was killed in a freak accident on his way to work one morning. Getting behind the wheel is one of life's most dangerous activities. If driving were a food, the U.S. Food and Drug Administration would regulate it out of existence tomorrow. Yet when was the last time you hesitated when you got behind the wheel because you were afraid of being hurt or killed? That's because we trust ourselves as drivers, which incidentally plays into the next influence on risk acceptance.

This explains why establishing trust with someone who is angry, worried, and suspicious is so vitally important. People feel that way in part because they think we're imposing a risk on them. Real or perceived, it doesn't matter. If they trust us as a source of that risk, they're 2,000 times more likely to accept it. That means they will be less angry, worried, and suspicious, and we will be more successful in winning them over.

Control and Understanding

Two powerful influences on risk acceptance, control and under-standing, often work in tandem. Along with trust, control helps to explain why we don't hesitate to drive. When most of us get behind the wheel, we feel we are in control. In August 2011, the insurance company Allstate asked 1,000 Americans to rate themselves as drivers. Close to two-thirds, 64 percent, rated themselves as excellent or very good drivers. Most of us think, "I'm a very good driver, and as long as I'm careful, I'll be fine." Anyone going slower than us is a moron. Anyone going faster is a maniac. We're Goldilocks behind the wheel; everything we do is just right. Perception versus reality comes into play here, too. The truth is, we don't have as much control as we think. Many people killed in car accidents are doing nothing wrong. They're simply in the wrong place at the wrong time when someone else does something wrong.

Many people who are afraid to fly cite a lack of control as a primary reason for their fear. Courses designed to alleviate these fears are built in part around helping fearful flyers understand how a plane works and what pilots do. While understanding does not equal personal control (those who take these courses won't be able to fly the plane), it does mitigate the *perception of the risk. When the plane goes up or down or left or right* or experiences turbulence, they'll know why and how. They'll have greater confidence that the pilots truly are in control, on their behalf. When we're trying to win people over, we need to raise their level of understanding of whatever risk they believe we're imposing on them. It's not enough to say, "Don't be afraid, because we'll take care of it."

I learned the hard way that the strategies, skills, and techniques necessary to break through and win people over can be important even when dealing with young children. I have two kids, an older son and a younger daughter. Before my daughter was born, my ex-wife and I did a lousy job of preparing my then four-year-old son for his sister's arrival. Sure, he knew she was coming and that he was going to have a little sister. But I never explained what that was really going to mean. That the baby would cry a lot. That she was going to sleep in Mommy and Daddy's room until she was old enough for her crib. That Mommy and Daddy would have to pay a lot of attention to her. That sort of thing. After his sister arrived, my son experienced awful night terrors. Looking back, I should have recognized that even at four—in a very subconscious way, to be sure—he felt that a new sister imposed a huge emotional burden on him. I'm convinced the transition would have been much easier had I helped him understand how a little baby in the house was going to change things and given him a sense of control over the situation.

By the way, the lifetime risk of being killed in an airplane (or space-related) accident is about 1 in 5,000. Driving is roughly 60 times more dangerous than flying. Which scares you more? Does control or understanding have something to do with it? Research shows that a sense of control can increase the willingness to accept a risk by as much as 1,000 times. Understanding is not quite so powerful, but it's an important factor, too.

Benefits

Many years ago, I worked with an organization that represents medical professionals who use small amounts of radioactive isotopes to diagnose and treat disease. At one of the group's meetings, a local television station asked one of its board members for an interview about a controversy involving a common medical procedure. Let's call the board member Dr. Pierce. Regulators recently had decided that the procedure wasn't effective and that insurance companies would no longer be required to cover it. The society believed the procedure was effective and wanted to overturn the decision—or at least convince people they should consider paying for it themselves even if their insurance wouldn't pay for it. In helping him to prepare, I urged Dr. Pierce to spend as much time as possible talking about the procedure's benefits. For the people watching the TV program, the risk was an emotional burden in the form of a financial liability: if I have this procedure, it's going to cost me a lot more now that my insurance won't cover it anymore. But if people recognize the benefits of a risk, research shows that they will be as much as 1,000 times more likely to accept it.

This was only part of the challenge, of course. Dr. Pierce also had to convince people that the procedure was effective, contrary to the recent regulatory ruling. But before he could win people over to that argument, he had to break through by identifying, acknowledging, and minimizing his audience's perceived risk. He also had to be careful about the nonverbal messages he was sending. We'll visit with Dr. Pierce again when we explore the importance of nonverbal messages in Chapter 6.

Choice v. Force

Most people are about 500 times more likely to accept a risk if they choose—or volunteer—for it, rather than being forced into it. The choice v. force factor plays a strong role in our perceived risk of driving. No one coerces us to get behind the wheel. We choose to drive. That's not true for many risks. If an electric company decides to build a power line in the field behind your house, that's hardly voluntary. Chances are you're going to perceive that power line as a risk on many different levels: power lines are ugly, so they'll ruin your view (an emotional burden); some studies find that power lines may negatively affect property value (a financial risk, another form of emotional burden); and other studies suggest electric and magnetic fields generated by power lines can be harmful (a physical threat).

To overcome the choice v. force factor, it's crucial to give members of the community many chances to be heard. We counsel our siting clients to hold numerous public meetings and information fairs, maintain open and frequent contact with community leaders, and provide numerous channels (e-mail addresses, phone numbers, etc.) that people can use to ask questions and provide input. Some people will oppose a controversial new facility no matter what, of course. But many, if given the opportunity to express their opinions and share their concerns, are more open-minded. They may not necessarily volunteer to host a new facility (although that can happen, especially if multiple communities are competing for the economic development and jobs—in other words, benefits!—that a facility will bring), but they will become more willing to accept the risks associated with it. And that will make it easier to win them over.

You don't have to be in the business of siting controversial facilities to use this risk acceptance factor to your advantage. Say you're giving an employee a challenging new assignment, something you know will test her abilities. Though positive, that's a risk in the form of an emotional burden. Instead of starting off by saying, "I have a challenging assignment for you," try asking, "Are you interested in taking on a challenging new assignment?" Now you're not imposing the risk. You're giving her a choice, and an opportunity to volunteer. Ninety-nine times out of a hundred, her answer is going be yes. And if her answer is no, well, then it may be time for a different sort of conversation.

Fairness and Equity

Research by Slovic and Gray and others shows that risks that affect many people are more acceptable than risks that affect only a few. Compare two of the risks we've discussed: driving a car and living near a power line. Driving affects just about everyone. The risk, though very high, is shared widely and equitably. Any one of us can be the victim of a bad, even fatal, car accident. The risk associated with living near a power line, while very low, affects only the people who live near it. From their point of view, they're bearing a disproportionate share of the risk. It's not fair. Like the choice v. force factor, fairness and equity can affect risk acceptance by as much as 500-fold. Interestingly, it's not only the few people affected by the risk who feel this way. Even those not affected directly will be less likely to accept a risk imposed on a select few.

When trying to win people over, ask these questions: Are you imposing an inequitable risk? How are people going to react? What can you do to make it fairer? The challenging job assignment may represent an unfair risk, from the employee's point of view. She may wonder why she's being singled out, even if you see it as a career-advancing opportunity. To overcome this concern, you need to empathize with her (more on this critical skill in Chapter 5). Provide her with the tools she'll need to do the job. Tell her you picked her because you know she can get it done, and that you'll be there to help her and allow her to ask questions. Not only will the conversation be easier, but the chances that she'll complete the assignment successfully will be much higher than if you simply said, "Go do this."

Familiarity

A couple of years ago I took up flying. The first lesson is called a demo flight. After my instructor took me through preflight (a 10-minute process during which he showed me how to check everything from the amount of gas in the tanks to the air pressure in the tires), we climbed into the cockpit. We ran through a prestart checklist, and he showed me how to start the engine. Then he turned to me and over the whine of the propeller very calmly said, "OK, taxi out to the runway and take off." I looked at him like he was crazy, but he assured me he wouldn't let me do anything wrong or dangerous. I was sweating. My heart was pounding. I've never been so nervous and worried—not to mention a little suspicious of a flight instructor who would let me "drive" a plane on my first day. In the end, everything went well, and as the plane lifted off the ground, all my angst disappeared. After a few months, I soloed. I no longer feared preflight or taxiing or taking off. I didn't really think about it at all. Climbing into the cockpit and taking off became as familiar as getting behind the wheel of my car. (In fact, driving got to be a little boring after I had experienced three-dimensional, traffic-free,

120-mile-per-hour travel.) What I had perceived to be a very big risk melted away in part thanks to familiarity—and in part to a sense of control and understanding.

Because people tend to fear the unknown, familiarity has a strong influence over risk acceptance: If we are familiar with a risk, we're 200 times more willing to accept it. Smart companies that operate controversial facilities recognize the power of familiarity. My firm has done work for a big energy company in New York charged with cleaning up an abandoned, contaminated site. The cleanup was controversial, with some residents accusing the company of making things worse rather than better. We counseled our client to be more proactive in reaching out to the community. The company brought local officials to the site and showed them what they were doing. They launched a new, more user-friendly website. They invited reporters to a big public meeting at the town's high school. By raising residents' familiarity with their operations, the company reduced their fear.

Publicity

Remember the movie *Jaws*? Released almost 40 years ago, it single-handedly raised shark attacks to the very top of the nation's collective list of things to fear. Beach resorts on every coast reported lower attendance that summer, and to this day, people hum the movie's iconic theme song and make jokes when they swim in the ocean. Media at the time picked up on the public's new fascination and began to report shark attack stories from all over the world. They still do.

When *Jaws* came out in 1975, the lifetime risk of being attacked by a shark was about 1 in 60,000—even less than being shot by the snipers in Washington, D.C. Today, the lifetime risk of being attacked by a shark is about 1 in 60,000. In other words, the real risk hasn't changed at all. What changed was the perceived risk, fueled by massive publicity launched and sustained by one very successful summer blockbuster movie.

As it turns out, sharks are not even close to the greatest risk you face when you spend a day at the beach. Driving there represents by far the biggest danger. The risk of drowning is about 1 in 1,100, while the risk of dying as a result of sun or heat exposure is about 1 in 13,000. And if you decide to take a bike ride: 1 in 5,000. Chances are none of these will happen to you, but a shark attack is the least of your worries.

Origin

Research clearly shows that people fear human-made risks more than natural ones. While I haven't seen any specific studies addressing it, I've always believed that this factor played into the controversy several years ago regarding the measles, mumps, and rubella (MMR) vaccine and autism. It started with the publication of a 1998 study in the well-respected medical journal *Lancet* that purported to show a connection between the two. The article spread like wildfire, and parents around the world began to refuse the vaccination. The only problem was that the study was completely wrong. Subsequent studies found no connection, and while the authors of the original *Lancet* article ultimately retracted it, the damage was done. To this day, a significant number of parents refuse the MMR vaccine, putting their children at much greater risk of contracting one of the diseases. In fact, even if the *Lancet* study had been proven true, the greater risk still would have been to go without the shot. The fact that the viruses that cause measles, mumps, and rubella are natural while humans created the vaccine that protects against them must, in my opinion, have played a role in this particular misperception of risk. Research shows that origin can influence risk acceptance by a factor of 200.

Dread

Risks that generate inordinate amounts of fear also can affect risk acceptance by a factor of 200. As I've mentioned, my firm does a lot of work in the nuclear power industry. We've learned that one risk that creates dread for many people is radiation. It's invisible and insidious, and one of the enduring images of the 20th century is of mushrooms clouds rising high into the sky. The March 11, 2011, Fukushima nuclear plant disaster in Japan reminded everyone of the dangers of radiation. Tens of thousands of people living near the plant were forced from their homes not by the earthquake or the tsunami, but by radiation leaking from the broken plant.

Radiation also serves to illustrate how different risk factors can work for and against one another. We fear what I'll call atomic radiation because it inspires dread, but also because it's human-made. The truth is we're exposed to radiation all the time from natural sources all around us, including radon in the ground and energy from the sun. But we tend not to worry about those nearly as much. We receive a relatively significant amount of radiation when we get x-rays on our teeth, but when was the last time you worried about the lead apron that the technician draped across you before he took the x-ray—or the fact that he stepped out of the room before pushing the button? Perhaps because you trust your dentist and you recognize the benefits associated with dental x-rays? Another time when many of us expose ourselves to relatively high levels of radiation is when we fly, because we rise above a good portion of the protective shield that the earth's atmosphere provides. I've never heard anyone cite radiation exposure among the reasons that they're afraid to fly, but a case could be made that the radiation you receive on a plane is the most dangerous part of the trip. I could go on and on, but you get the idea.

Children and Future Generations

As Paul Slovic has written, because we are genetically programmed to care for our children, we are far less willing to accept risks we believe affect them disproportionately. This factor played a strong role in the Alar scare of the late 1980s. Alar was a chemical that farmers used to make apples stay ripe longer, until the Natural Resources Defense Council issued a report declaring it to be an unacceptable risk to children. Parents all over the country erupted in fury. They forced stores to pull apples and apple products from their shelves and schools to stop using them in lunches served to students. In the end, their reaction turned out to be way out of proportion to the risk. Once the initial furor subsided, many studies, including one published in 1990 in the official journal of the National Academy of Sciences, concluded that Alar was perfectly safe. But the real risk didn't have a chance against a perceived threat aimed primarily at children, and the chemical is banned from use on food products to this day.

Concerns about children can be so powerful that we're even less likely to accept risks that may affect future generations. Depending on whether we have children and how old they are, this factor can affect risk acceptance by a factor of 200 to 1,000.

Catastrophic Potential

We tend to fear risks that threaten to cause a large number of casualties all at once more than those that result in the same number of casualties spread out over a longer period of time. That's why studies show that most of us fear terrorist attacks like the ones that occurred on September 11, 2001, more than we do random street crime. We're much more likely to worry about the former, even though we're much more likely to suffer from the latter—even in cities high on the target list of terrorists, including Washington, D.C. Risk acceptance can be affected 500-fold by this influence factor.

How Nonrisks Become Imminent Danger, and Vice Versa

To close out our risk primer, let's engage in an exercise that will show how these risk factors change perceived risks into real risks. We'll compare driving and living next to a power line. We know that the real risk associated with driving is about 1 in 100. I couldn't find a reliable statistic on the risk associated with living near a power line, probably because it's so low, but for the sake of argument, let's say it's 1 in 100,000. That's even less of a risk than the one posed by the snipers (or by sharks).

Start with trust. Do we trust ourselves behind the wheel? Yes. As the Allstate study tells us, most of us consider ourselves to be excellent or very good drivers. So what happens to our perception of the risk of driving? Because we trust the risk of driving, our perception of the risk goes down by a factor of 2,000.

So a real risk of 1 in 100 becomes, in our minds, a perceived risk of 1 in 200,000. In other words, the trust factor leads us to believe that driving is 2,000 times safer than it really is.

Now consider the power line. Do we trust the company that wants to build it? Probably not. Power companies are big, faceless corporations that only care about making money, or so we think. They'll do and say whatever it takes to get the line built. They don't really care if the line is safe or not. Besides, power lines are big, ugly, and scary. Since we don't trust the source of this risk, our perception of the risk goes up by a factor of 2,000. Rather than a risk of 1 in 100,000, we perceive the risk to be more like 1 in 50—or 2,000 times riskier than it really is.

Look what happened. By applying only one of the factors that influence risk, we turned the very real risk of driving into a perceived risk that's less likely than a shark attack, being hit by lightning, or even being killed in a fireworks-related accident! The opposite happened when we applied the trust factor to living near a power line. What is actually very safe became, essentially, an imminent danger.

Applying other factors such as benefits, familiarity, and control would only make driving seem safer and living next to a power line seem even more dangerous. In fact, many people who live along a proposed new power line's route will just assume that if it gets built, they're going to die. That's why so many people fight so hard to stop the construction of controversial facilities that will almost surely do them no harm, but so few give driving a second thought.

Think about some of the other risks we've discussed. How do these factors play into the fear of flying? Or terrorism attacks? Or smoking? Which ones make the perceived risks higher? And which make them lower?

THE RISK OF RISK COMPARISONS

People become angry, worried, and suspicious when they believe a risk is being imposed on them. We may know that the risk isn't real or at least that it's very small. But that doesn't matter. If people *perceive* the risk to be high, we have to communicate with them as if it were real. Later in the book, we're going to explore traps that people fall into when trying to win people over, and how to avoid or escape those traps. It's appropriate to preview one of them here: the trap of risk comparisons. In tough situations, communicators often try to compare the risk they're imposing with something more familiar in an attempt to make people feel better. This can easily backfire, and we'll discuss how to handle risk comparisons in Chapter 9.

Now that you understand how people assess risk and how that plays into the all-important equation of perception equals reality, it's time to begin exploring at the strategies, skills, and techniques that will help you win over people when they're angry, worried, and suspicious of everything you say. In the next chapter, we'll look at the criteria by which people judge whether or not you're trustworthy and credible, and you'll begin to learn what you can do to make sure the answer is yes.

Chapter 5

THE CODE FOR TRUST AND CREDIBILITY

How to Get It, Keep It, and Use It

People don't care how much you know until they know how much you care.

— UNKNOWN

S everal years ago, a power plant in the Midwest released a small amount of hazardous waste into a local lake. As you can imagine, the incident generated a lot of concern. Hundreds of people live along the lake's shores. Thousands flock to it during the summer to swim, fish, and water-ski. Local officials, bombarded with calls from residents demanding to know whether they were in any danger, summoned an executive from the utility that owned the plant to a public meeting at the local high school. Let's call the executive Mr. Malone. They also invited a professor from a nearby university to assess the spill and speak about any potential threat it posed to the community.

That night, several hundred angry, worried, and suspicious people packed the high school auditorium. They didn't have any reason to trust Mr. Malone. After all, he represented a big, faceless corporation they perceived to be interested only in the bottom line. Beyond those who worked there, few people perceived any tangible benefits from having the plant operate just a few miles from their homes. They lacked any control over the situation, and almost no one understood how the plant operated. They believed that the leak threatened the children who swam in the lake. In other words, nearly every one of the major risk assessment factors we discussed in Chapter 4 drove the crowd to believe that the leak represented an imminent danger.

Mr. Malone faced a very tough situation. He knew the leak was extremely small and posed no threat to people or the environment, but in order to break through and win people over, he knew he had to establish himself as a trustworthy and credible source of information.

The professor spoke first. He spent 30 minutes running through a dizzying array of facts about the situation, including the amount and toxicity of the waste that spilled into the lake, likely dispersal patterns, and potential exposure metrics. He stood behind the podium as he spoke, referring to slides with lots of numbers and complex graphs. He used big, complicated, technical words that few people in the audience understood. By the time he finished, the crowd was even angrier and more worried and suspicious. (This is a good example, by the way, of how the local credibility we discussed in Chapter 2 doesn't always hold if someone makes too many other mistakes.)

When it was his turn to speak, Mr. Malone took the microphone off the podium and stepped down from the stage so he stood level with the crowd. He began by saying how happy he was to be standing in the auditorium again and how it brought back a lot of fond memories from the days when his three kids attended the school. For the next several minutes, he reminisced about high school plays, proms, and sporting events. He told the audience that while he hadn't been to the school in a long time, he and his wife still lived just a few blocks away. In fact, he said, he and his wife had walked to the meeting. He explained how they had come early so they could spend a little time catching with old friends. He also told them that he looked forward to reconnecting with the school, because one of his daughters also lived in the neighborhood, and he expected that his young grandchildren would eventually roam its halls as his own children once had.

Only then did Mr. Malone start talking about the spill. For no more than 10 minutes, he explained what had happened, using simple, plain language. He accepted full responsibility for the spill, for cleaning it up, and for making sure it never happened again. He closed with the following statement:

> I understand that many of you are concerned about what happened at my plant. I'm concerned, too, and I'm going to do whatever it takes to figure out exactly what happened and fix it and to make sure this is the last time

anything like this ever happens again. When it's fixed, I'll tell you what we did and why. You know, I live here. And my family lives here. I'll tell you the same thing I told my daughter when she asked if she should be worried about her family's safety: the spill was unfortunate, but it was very small. We've conducted many tests, including immediately after it happened, and we have been unable to detect any trace of the spill. Which is why I was very comfortable telling my daughter that she and her kids are perfectly safe. So are all of you and your kids.

That's my main message to you: you and your kids are safe. You can swim in the lake, as my wife and I did just last weekend. You can fish. You can water-ski.

Now I'm sure you have many questions, and I'll stay as long as it takes to answer them. And I have a stack of my business cards up here with me. When the meeting is over, feel free to come up and talk to me individually and to grab a card so you know how to reach me if you have any questions or concerns after you've gone home.

Then he sat down. In less than 15 minutes, Mr. Malone had turned an angry, worried, and suspicious crowd poised to attack him into a relieved, appreciative group of concerned but calm residents. When the moderator opened the floor for Q&A, they pelted the professor with difficult, hostile questions for almost an hour. Mr. Malone barely said another word.

I'm proud to tell you that Mr. Malone succeeded in part because my firm helped him prepare for the meeting. Everything he said and did, from walking to the school to talking about his family to bringing business cards to hand out to people, was designed to prove to the assembled parents that he was trustworthy and credible. He succeeded in winning over the crowd because he employed the right strategies, skills, and techniques.

FOUR CRITERIA THAT GOVERN THE PERCEPTION OF TRUST AND CREDIBILITY

Learning to succeed as Mr. Malone did begins with understanding how people judge whether you're a trustworthy and credible person. Research conducted by Dr. Vincent Covello at the Center for Risk Communication has revealed that most people base that judgment on four criteria:

1. Caring and empathy
2. Openness and honesty
3. Dedication and commitment
4. Expertise and competence

Figure 5.1 offers a powerful example.

In normal situations, people don't judge you at all, so these criteria don't matter. As we discussed earlier, absent a risk that sparks anger, worry, and suspicion, the vast majority of people with whom you communicate assume you're a trustworthy and credible person. You don't have to pay any attention to caring or honesty or dedication, because the people with whom you're communicating aren't paying any attention to them.

That all changes in a tough situation. When people perceive a risk and become angry, worried, and suspicious, they immedi-

FIGURE 5.1 World War II Victors—and Great Communicators

Great communicators succeed in large part because they personify the four criteria that people use to judge trust and credibility: caring and empathy, openness and honesty, dedication and commitment, and expertise and competence. Successful politicians are particularly adept at communicating all four. Franklin Roosevelt connected with Americans suffering through the Great Depression and the Second World War by telling caring and empathetic stories that showed he understood what they were going through. Winston Churchill covered all four when he uttered his famous line about the war against Nazi Germany upon becoming prime minister of Great Britain in 1940: "I have nothing to offer but blood, toil, tears and sweat." In 11 words, he showed himself to be caring, honest, committed, and competent.

ately and continuously assess and monitor everything you say and do through the filter of these four criteria. People don't necessarily know that they're doing it. It happens subconsciously. And that filter causes them to view every signal you send, verbally and otherwise, in the most negative way possible.

Sweating is a good example. Let's say you have to give a speech to 200 colleagues and peers. Chances are you're going to be nervous. According to many studies, including one conducted in 2006 by Dr. Paul L. Witt, an assistant professor of communication studies at Texas Christian University, public speaking is the number one fear reported by Americans. It's the basis of one of Jerry Seinfeld's most famous jokes: "According to most studies, people's number one fear is public speaking. Number two is death. Death is number two. Does that sound right? This means to the average person, if you go to a funeral, you're better off in the casket than doing the eulogy."

If you're nervous and anxious, you may start to sweat. That's perfectly normal. If you have to use a handkerchief to mop your brow during the speech, your colleagues and peers won't hold it against you. They'll think, "He's nervous, just like I would be." Or they might think the lights are hot. But turn those 200 colleagues and peers into 200 angry, worried, and suspicious members of a community where your company just leaked even a small amount of hazardous waste into a lake, and they won't give you that benefit of the doubt. They'll view the fact that you're sweating through a negative filter. You're not sweating because you're nervous. You're sweating because you don't want to be there. Or you're trying to hide something. Or you're lying.

Knowing this has led our firm to give up a lot for our clients (see Figure 5.2).

Angry, worried, and suspicious people pay attention not only to what you say but also to what you do with your eyes, hands, posture, clothing, and many other nonverbal cues (more on this in Chapter 6). To win them over, you have to send all the

FIGURE 5.2 Sweating and the Shirts off Our Backs

In 2005, one of the partners in my firm traveled to New Orleans right after Hurricane Katrina came through and devastated the city. He met one of our clients to shoot video of some of the damage. It was hot and muggy, and after a couple of hours, the client, who was narrating the video, sweated right through his shirt. Knowing that in a tough situation, angry, worried, and suspicious people will interpret sweating as a sign of dishonesty, my partner literally gave the client the shirt off his back.

right signals. Then they will be willing to hear what you have to say, believe what you have to say, and ultimately act on what you have to say. If you send any of the wrong signals—just one!—they may decide you are neither trustworthy nor credible. Even if you show that you're caring, open, and dedicated, you will fail if they don't perceive you to be an expert. Which means you might as well pack up and go home, because nothing you say will be heard or believed or acted upon.

Now that you see how important these factors are, let's take a look at each of them in turn, discussing what you need to do to send the right signals and establish yourself as a trustworthy and credible source of information.

CARING AND EMPATHY

Research shows that of the criteria people use to judge trust and credibility, caring and empathy are by far the most important. When people are angry, worried, and suspicious, most will decide whether you're a caring and empathetic person *within 30 seconds of meeting you.* And once they have made a decision, it's nearly impossible to change their minds. That puts a premium on making an immediate impression, which means the first thing out of your mouth in tough situations must be caring and empathetic.

What is caring and empathy? The best and most relevant definition I've read comes from the popular book *Difficult Conversations: How to Discuss What Matters Most,* published in 1999. Here's how authors Douglas Stone, Bruce Patton, and Sheila Heen describe empathy (and, in essence, caring as well):

The deepest form of understanding another person is empathy. Empathy involves a shift from my observing how you seem on the outside, to my imagining what it feels like to be you on the inside, wrapped in your skin with your set of experiences and background, looking at the world through your eyes. . . . Psychologists have found that we are each more interested in knowing that the other person is trying to empathize with us—that they are willing to struggle to understand how we feel and see how we see—than we are in believing that they have accomplished that goal.

Caring and empathy come in different forms. Risk communication expert Peter Sandman argues that it's not enough to acknowledge an audience's concerns or simply to show we're paying attention. He believes caring and empathy must be communicated in a respectful, gentle way. In tough situations, the best—and really only—way to do that well is to tell a personal story.

Notice that Mr. Malone didn't start his speech by trying to explain the spill or why it happened, as the professor did. Instead, he talked about the school and his family. He shared memories and expressed feelings that showed the people in the auditorium that he was just like them, implying that he shared their thoughts and concerns. In his audience's eyes, he became more than an executive with the company responsible for the spill. He was a husband, a father, and a concerned member of the community. He lived there. So did his daughter, and her children. When he spoke, he didn't stand behind a podium or talk down to the people in the auditorium from a platform. He stepped down to their level. He put himself in their shoes and showed them in words and in actions that he understood them and their feelings. By demonstrating that he was a caring and empathetic person first and a utility executive second, Mr. Malone went a long way toward establishing trust and credibility with his angry, worried, and suspicious audience.

As it turns out, he went about halfway. Research shows that caring or empathy accounts for about half of the trust and credibility judgment that people will make of you. My firm has organized the four trust and credibility criteria into what we call a "CODE score." Figure 5.3 lists the criteria and the number of points my firm has assigned to each. As you can see, the caring and empathy criterion accounts for 50 points. Each of the other criteria—openness and honesty, dedication and commitment, and expertise and competence—accounts for 10 to 15 points. Add them all up, and a perfect CODE score is 100. When my firm trains people such as Mr. Malone, we push them hard to earn a perfect score. Anything less, even a 95, means they may fail to establish trust and credibility. And if they fail to establish trust and credibility, they'll never be able to break through and win people over.

It's not enough simply to tell people that you understand their feelings or share their concerns. You have to *prove* it to them. That's what personal stories do. They resonate much more powerfully than simply saying you're sorry.

In the previous chapter, I mentioned my partner who lost a job early in his career. Here's what he actually said to one of the employees we had to let go:

FIGURE 5.3 The CODE Score for Trust and Credibility

Caring & Empathy	+	Openness & Honesty	+	Dedication & Commitment	+	Expertise & Competence	=	Total Score
50 points		15–20 points		15–20 points		15–20 points		100 points

Based on four criteria identified by Dr. Vincent Covello at the Center for Risk Communication, my firm developed what we call a CODE score for remembering and measuring success in establishing trust and credibility. By demonstrating that you're caring, open, dedicated, and expert, you'll be able to break through and win people over. Any score less than 100 means you may fail, so it's crucial that you do everything exactly right when your audience is angry, worried, and suspicious.

Barbara Longsworth

This happened to me when I was about your age. It was really hard, but I bounced back from it. In fact, losing that job put me on the track to getting this job, and I'm much happier here. So I have a sense of what you're feeling right now. I'm sorry you have to go through it, but I know from personal experience that everything will work out just fine.

It immediately defused a potentially tough situation and actually put the employee at ease. It was still a difficult meeting, but my partner's caring and empathetic story made it much easier for everyone.

When I teach classes on how to win people over in tough situations, people often stop me at this point and ask, "What happens if I don't have any stories?" My response is always the same: "If you really think about it, you probably have more than you realize. And if you don't, go get some." Obviously you can't lay yourself off if that hasn't happened to you. But it probably has happened to someone you know and care about—a relative or a friend. If you're in a position where you may have to let people go, talk to people you know who've gone through it. It's not quite the same as being able to say you've been there yourself, but it's much better than simply saying, "I'm sorry." For clients who represent their organizations out in the community—whatever community that may be—I encourage them to get out of their offices and talk to people. Walk the factory floor and chat with colleagues. Join a local business group, and get to know your neighbors and peers. You'll pick up a lot of stories just by walking around and talking to people, which is something you should be doing anyway!

One last note: Caring and empathy must be genuine. While caring and empathy may be the most powerful of the four trust and credibility criteria, the others also are important. It's not effective, nor is it ethical, to feign caring and empathy in order to manipulate people. If you're not a caring and empathetic person or don't feel that way in a particular situation, find someone else to communicate on your behalf.

OPENNESS AND HONESTY

No matter what, effective communicators must tell the truth. Being deceitful or trying to hide something *always* backfires, and once you're caught, you're done. You'll never establish trust and credibility. The criterion of openness and honesty accounts for roughly one-fifth of your CODE score, or between 15 and 20 points.

Mr. Malone earned openness and honesty points when he admitted that his company was still trying to figure out exactly why the leak at his plant had occurred. He promised to find out and to share the information with the community as soon as he had it. The same principle applies if you have to explain a mistake to your boss. Don't beat around the bush. After you've expressed caring and empathy, explain exactly what happened and why. Take responsibility, promise to figure out what went wrong, and describe what you're going to do to prevent it from happening again. The conversation will be much easier, and chances are the ramifications, if any, will be less severe.

This is something politicians never seem to remember. Rather than admitting the truth and accepting responsibility, they too often resort to obfuscation and cover-ups, an approach that rarely works out well. My dad often shares an anecdote about a television interview that George H. W. Bush gave after losing a primary race he had been expected to win during the 1980 presidential election. The reporter asked the future vice president and president why he thought he lost. Bush replied, "I have no idea what happened, but we'd better figure it out, or we're going to be in big trouble." With this surprising and disarming candor, Bush earned at least one lifelong fan and supporter—and spent the next 12 years in the White House.

Unlike too many politicians, you, I hope, find it obvious that breaking through and winning people over depends on telling the truth. What may be less obvious is that it also depends on *showing* the truth. When it comes to openness and honesty, you have to send the right nonverbal messages. We'll cover this in more detail in the next chapter, but in part that means:

▶ *Making good eye contact with your audience.* In determining whether or not you are trustworthy and credible, people pay closest attention to what you're doing with your eyes. Anything other than maximum eye contact sends negative signals that angry, worried, and suspicious people will interpret as being deceptive.

▶ *Removing barriers from between you and your audience.* Mr. Malone got out from behind the podium on the stage of the high school auditorium in part to send the signal that he had nothing to hide. If you have to discipline an employee, don't sit behind your desk. Come around and sit in a chair.

▶ *Showing your hands when you speak.* Hiding your hands in any way—behind your back, in your pockets, or even clasped together—sends the message that you're holding back or concealing something.

Finally, it's perfectly acceptable to follow the example set by Mr. Malone and the first President Bush and admit that you don't know something. The people I teach often worry about not being able to remember an important fact or the answer to an obvious question. If you don't know, say so—but promise to follow up. Here's a ready-made response you can use:

> That's a very good question, but the answer escapes me at the moment. Let me have your phone number. I'll find out the answer and get back to you no later than the end of the day tomorrow.

Make sure you keep your promise to follow up, or you'll lose dedication and commitment points. You also can't fall back on this response too often. Otherwise, you'll undercut the expertise and competence portion of your score.

DEDICATION AND COMMITMENT

Whether you're disciplining an employee, trying to make up after a fight with your significant other, or speaking to a hostile group of people, it's essential to show them that you're reaching out and communicating not because you *have* to, but because you *want* to. Demonstrating that kind of dedication and com-

mitment to addressing people's concerns and taking them seriously account for another 15 to 20 percent of your CODE score.

Mr. Malone scored dedication and commitment points in
several ways. He and his wife came to the meeting early. They
took the opportunity to greet people in the audience ahead
of time, which likely defused some of their anger, worry, and
suspicion before the meeting formally began. He talked about
his roots in the community and made it clear that he was just
as determined to figure out what had happened and to fix it as
anyone in the room. As he said, he and his family lived there
too, after all. He brought personal business cards and invited
everyone to take one and to call him directly if they had questions. That may seem like a big time commitment for a busy
executive, but I can tell you that no one ever called. Just the fact
that Mr. Malone was willing to give out his contact information
was enough for the people in the audience. When the meeting ended, Mr. Malone and his wife didn't rush out the door.
They stayed, greeting more people and answering more of what
I call quiet questions. People who left right away and looked
over their shoulders saw Mr. Malone standing at the front of the
auditorium and chatting with people, rather than rushing out.
He was sending a very strong signal to everyone: I'm not here
because I have to be. I'm here because I want to be.

In tough situations, let your audience decide when the interaction is over, as Al Gore did during his presidential campaign in
2000 (see Figure 5.4). Give them an opportunity to ask as many
questions as they want, and make sure they have a way to get in
touch with you afterward if they have any additional questions

or concerns. Chances are they won't, but you'll earn the full 15 to 20 dedication and commitment points of your CODE score.

Many clients with whom I work ask whether it's appropriate to provide personal contact information. That really depends

FIGURE 5.4 Al Gore Stays and Scores

Presidential candidates typically rush from one event to another with little regard for what their late arrivals and early departures do to their CODE scores. They get away with it for two reasons: people expect that kind of behavior from politicians, and, in most cases, they aren't operating in tough situations where the rules for winning people over apply. Nevertheless, during the 2000 campaign, Vice President Al Gore stayed at a number of campaign town hall meetings until everyone else had left. Ultimately, it wasn't enough to win him the White House, but several papers ran front-page stories on Gore's dedication to his audiences and his commitment to hearing their concerns and answering their questions.

on the particular situation and your own comfort level. In most cases, a work phone number or e-mail address will suffice, but feel free to go the extra mile if it feels right (and safe).

EXPERTISE AND COMPETENCE

The good news about the final criterion, expertise and competence, is that these 15 to 20 expertise points are the easiest to earn. Even Mr. Malone, who walked into the high school with very little trust and credibility, began the evening with a CODE score of about 20 points. He needed to work hard to earn his caring, openness, and dedication points, but the angry, worried, and suspicious residents who filled the auditorium that night undoubtedly gave him the benefit of the doubt when it came to his expertise. He was, after all, a top executive with the utility that owned the power plant. He had the experience, competence, and education to attain a high position in his company. Surely he must know what he's talking about.

Chances are you'll get the same benefit of the doubt when you step into a tough situation and seek to win people over. Your audience, whether one person or many, will at the very least believe you have a certain level of expertise. What they'll wonder is whether you're going to empathize with them, tell them the truth, and commit yourself to addressing their concerns.

The bad news about expertise and competence is that this criterion accounts for only 15 to 20 percent of your CODE score, and, because it's largely assumed, the only direction to go is down. We already discussed one of the quickest ways to lose expertise points: saying you don't know too often. Another common mistake is to throw around a lot of jargon. My partners and I work with a lot of very smart people who represent very complicated industries. We often struggle to scrub acronyms and confusing terminology from their vocabulary. They throw these terms around all the time with no trouble when speaking to colleagues and peers. But when you're communicating with lay people who are angry, concerned, and suspicious of everything you say, jargon comes across not as intelligent but as condescending. Nontechnical people don't understand technical terms and have a hard time keeping up. That drives down your expertise and competence score. We'll touch on the jargon trap again in Chapter 9.

Think again about what Mr. Malone said. He was very careful not to repeat the professor's mistake of using terms like "parts per billion" or "exposure metrics." He spoke in clear, concise terms. He explained what had happened at the plant and what he was doing to fix it, using simple language that was understandable to the people in his audience, who had no idea how the plant operated. He didn't try to show how smart he was by using big words. And he didn't talk down to his listeners. He treated them with respect. As a result, he held on to the 20 expertise and competence points he had brought with him into the auditorium, even as he earned the other 80 caring and empathy, openness and honesty, and dedication and commitment points.

You can employ many other techniques to bolster your CODE scores. Because society perceives men and women differently when it comes to the four CODE criteria, some of these techniques differ depending on whether you're a man or a woman. In Chapter 7, we'll delve deeper into what you can do to boost your CODE score based on your gender. But before that, let's take a close look at an even more powerful determinant of your CODE score: nonverbal messages. How you say something is far more important than what you say when it comes to winning people over when they're angry, concerned, and suspicious of everything you say.

Chapter 6

NONVERBAL MESSAGES AND THEIR IMPACT ON THE CODE

What you do speaks so loud that I cannot hear what you say.

— RALPH WALDO EMERSON,
AMERICAN POET

Remember Dr. Pierce from Chapter 4? My firm helped him prepare for a television interview during which he discussed a government decision not to require insurance companies to cover a certain medical procedure. He was actually one of four experts who appeared on a panel during the interview. Although I fought against it for reasons that will become clear later, the station forced all four panelists to sit behind a table. Since I couldn't get Dr. Pierce out from behind it, I urged him to lean forward during the entire interview, with his forearms resting on the edge of the table and his hands open and pointed toward the camera.

He did an excellent job. Only once did he start to lean back, but before he could get all the way back, I caught his eye from behind the camera and started waving my arms frantically. He got the (nonverbal) message and leaned right back forward. The other three members of the panel leaned back in their chairs the entire time. One folded his arms across his chest. Another clasped his hands behind his head part of the time. The interview lasted about 10 minutes. The reporter asked Dr. Pierce one question, and it was a friendly, simple one that he knocked out of the park. The others got hammered with very difficult—and, in a few cases, even hostile—questions.

Maybe Dr. Pierce got lucky. But I would argue that he avoided the tough questions because he sent the right nonverbal messages to the reporter (and to the program's viewers). Because he sat forward, he showed that he was engaged—that he cared and was committed. By showing his hands, he sent a subtle psychological signal that he was being honest and open. Without saying a word, he drove his CODE score up toward 100. By employing all the right techniques, Dr. Pierce gave the reporter no reason to challenge or embarrass him. I believe the reporter fired tough questions at the other panelists mainly because their nonverbal cues made him at the very least suspicious, and perhaps even a little angry.

RESEARCH ON NONVERBAL MESSAGES GOES BACK 40 YEARS

Modern academic research on the ways in which nonverbal cues influence the perception of trust and credibility began in the late

1960s and early 1970s with the work of Dr. Albert Mehrabian at the University of California, Los Angeles. Mehrabian's original study, later expanded upon in his classic 1971 text, *Silent Messages*, concludes that the average person decides if he or she "likes" a person based on three factors: words, tone of voice, and facial expressions. The seminal study further assigns relative weight to each of those factors:

Total Liking = 7% Words + 38% Tone of Voice + 55% Facial Expressions

Essentially, Mehrabian concluded that when someone judges whether or not he or she likes you, the person pays more attention to how you sound and look than to what you say. In other words, what you communicate *visually* is more important than what you communicate verbally.

Over the past 40 years, researchers have built on this initial work. We've learned that people pay attention to a lot more than just tone of voice and facial expressions. Subconsciously, they evaluate hundreds of nonverbal cues as they determine whether they like someone or, for our purposes, whether they find someone to be trustworthy and credible.

We've also learned that while people constantly read nonverbal cues in every situation, they interpret and evaluate the cues differently depending on the nature of the relationship. Friends, family, and coworkers notice and process nonverbal cues but tend to give you the benefit of the doubt. You can stand behind a lectern, leave a shirttail untucked, or fold your hands behind your back—no big deal. In these normal situations, people tend to give you time to convince them that you're more than your negative nonverbal cues might suggest. In general, we go easy on the people we know and trust.

In tough situations, when people perceive that a risk is being imposed on them, they judge every nonverbal cue in the most negative way possible. (Remember our discussion of sweating and public speaking in Chapter 5.) And they judge very quickly, often in as little as 30 seconds—before you even have a chance to *say* anything. That's why it was essential that Dr. Pierce send the right nonverbal cues from the very beginning. The reporter and his audience were set to judge him long before he spoke. The consequences of negative nonverbal cues are so severe that even a spot on Dr. Pierce's tie would have driven his CODE score down. Not by much, perhaps. But when you're trying to break through and win people over, every point counts.

To have any chance to win people over when they're angry, worried, and suspicious of everything you say, you need to actively and deliberately send the right nonverbal messages if you want to have any chance to show that you're trustworthy and credible. Of all the strategies, skills, and techniques covered in this book, this may be the most difficult to master, because it takes both mind and body control. You have to pay attention to many different things, literally from your head to your toes. And you have to practice over and over again to figure out what things you're doing wrong and make them right.

THE BIG SEVEN NONVERBAL CUES

Through decades of research, both in the laboratory and the field, experts have identified seven nonverbal cues that rank as the most important:

1. Maintain eye contact.
2. Show the palms of your hands.
3. Maintain a neutral facial expression.
4. Adopt a stance that is firm, forward, and friendly.
5. Dress appropriately.
6. Arrive early and stay late.
7. Remove or step around any physical barriers.

Breaking through and winning people over requires understanding the Big Seven and doing them all just right.

One word of caution when it comes to nonverbal messages: the strategies, skills, and techniques we'll explore in this chapter are based on American culture. Other cultures will interpret and react to these nonverbal cues in very different ways. As I learned on a trip to Thailand, showing someone the bottom of your foot is considered very rude. Whenever you find yourself in an unfamiliar culture, make the effort to learn which nonverbal signals you should emphasize—and which you should avoid. If you ever find yourself in Beijing, say, trying to convince local officials to let you build an industrial facility, be sure to consult experts on Chinese culture and society, and refine your strategies, skills, and techniques accordingly.

EYES: THE WINDOWS TO THE SOUL— AND CREDIBILITY

You send and receive more nonverbal signals with your eyes than with any other body part. Eyes are the number one nonverbal cue that angry, worried, and suspicious people will use to determine whether you're trustworthy and credible.

Some researchers spend their entire careers studying the signals people send with their eyes, and dozens of books have been written about how they play into the way we judge trust and credibility. Here's just one example: When right-handed people *access* an existing image in their minds, they tend to look to the left or up and to the left, but when they *create* a new image in their minds, they tend to look to the right or up and to the right. The movement tends to be in the opposite direction for left-handed people. This suggests that when most people tell the truth, their eyes move *away* from their dominant hand. When they lie, their eyes move *toward* their dominant hand. As you can imagine, this is far from a perfect science. Not everyone behaves this way. But these eye movements can have a tremendous impact on people who are judging trust and credibility, because people who are angry, worried, and suspicious interpret these signals in the worst possible light.

Fortunately, you don't need to understand the complex intricacies of eye movement to succeed when it comes to this nonverbal cue. The trick to sending the right nonverbal messages with your eyes is simple: establish and maintain good eye contact. When you make good eye contact, you show that you care about your audience's feelings, that you respect audience members and their opinions, that you're there to listen, and that you're dedicated to addressing their concerns. (Some experts believe good eye contact also shows that you're honest, though others consider this to be an open question.) If you don't make good eye contact, you send all the opposite signals: that you don't care, don't respect your audience's feelings and opinions, and don't want to interact with audience members.

While establishing and maintaining good eye contact is essential whether you're addressing one person or a hundred, it's often easier said than done. With one person, the most effective technique is to maintain eye contact for as long as two or three minutes, and then to look away for a few seconds before locking back in. This sends the right signals without appearing to stare, which can be interpreted as rude or even threatening, especially when engaging in a tough situation.

Many people, including some of my most successful clients, struggle to maintain eye contact for two or three minutes at a time. Carol Kinsey Goman, an expert in nonverbal communication and author of *The Nonverbal Advantage*, offers a technique that can be very effective: Create an imaginary triangle on the face of the person with whom you're communicating, with the eyes as the bottom two corners and the middle of the forehead as the apex. If you look in this area (Goman calls this the "business gaze"), you get all the advantages of good eye contact without appearing to stare. Be careful, though. Goman warns that if you invert the triangle, with the eyes now as the *top* two corners, you've wandered into the "social gaze." If you look there, the nonverbal messages you send will be much different. Let's just say the social gaze is more appropriate in a bar than a business meeting.

Communicating with a group of people is a little more complicated, but for some, a little more comfortable, too. You should lock eyes with one person for several seconds, then break off and lock eyes with another person, and so on. You don't have to lock eyes with everyone in the room, and it's OK to go back to someone a second or even third time. The key is to keep moving from one person to the next.

In addition to all the other positive nonverbal messages Dr. Pierce sent, he maintained good eye contact with the reporter. And as I tell the people who ask me about television interviews, the reporter's face is precisely where you should look. The simple rule of thumb is to look at the reporter, employing the techniques we've discussed. The only setting where you should look at the camera is called a live-remote, where you're sitting alone in a room and listening to a reporter ask questions in your ear. In a live-remote, you should stare directly into the camera. More on that in Chapter 8.

Like most of the skills and techniques associated with winning people over, good eye contact takes plenty of practice. Don't be shy about asking your spouse or a friend to help you get it right.

HAVE YOUR AUDIENCE IN THE PALM OF YOUR HANDS

When I train people, one of the first things I look at is what they do with their hands when they talk. I specifically watch for one of the two extremes that can most affect trust and credibility: flailing hands that totally overwhelm what someone is saying, or motionless hands that make a person appear robotic. Fortunately, most people fall somewhere in between these two extremes. But even if you move your hands appropriately and comfortably, you can send the wrong signals in situations where people are angry, worried, and suspicious of everything you say.

Show Your Palms

When it comes to hands, remember my advice to Dr. Pierce: keep them visible to your audience at all times, and show your palms as often as possible. This gesture communicates deep, subconscious messages lodged in our collective psychology. Jesus Christ, who billions of people consider to have been the most trustworthy and credible person who ever lived, was nailed to the cross with his arms extended and his palms facing out. Religious leaders often spread their arms in front of them in a gesture meant to encompass and soothe (see Figure 6.1), and this nonverbal language remains effective despite the scandals that recently rocked the Catholic Church. The technique also traces back to the origin of the handshake, a custom that goes back at least to ancient Greece: when you show others your open palms, you confirm that you're not carrying a weapon. Today, visible hands and open palms suggest that you are caring, open, and dedicated—not to mention nonthreatening.

How should you show open palms? When you are standing, the best technique is to hold your hands in front your body, between your hips and your shoulders. Ideally, you'll keep your hands apart, but it's OK to occasionally touch your fingers together, as long as they are in front of you. Some people my firm trains ask if it's all right to hold something, like a pen, because they believe it calms them down. While this can be effective for people who suffer from "flailing hands," in general it's best to learn how to communicate without them. I've seen too many people who start to fiddle with what they're holding, which distracts from what they're saying.

FIGURE 6.1 Open Hands, Open Heart

When it comes to judging credibility, we take many of our nonverbal cues from trustworthy sources. Showing the palms of your hands conveys openness, honesty, and safety, in part because it's a gesture made frequently by religious leaders.

©iStockphoto.com/kati1313

One effective technique is to touch your heart. The heart embodies love, the soul, and life itself. Resting an open palm on your heart as you speak, when appropriate, sends a very strong signal of openness, dedication, and warmth.

What Not to Do

If keeping your hands in front of you, showing your palms as often as you can, and touching your heart represent what you should do, Figure 6.2 illustrates what you shouldn't do. Here's how these other hand positions affect your message in tough situations:

FIGURE 6.2 What You Say When You Hide Your Hands

Sticking your hands in your pockets

Holding your hands clasped behind your back

Clasping your hands below your beltline

Crossing your arms

Clasping your hands behind your head

Putting your hands on your hips

Wringing your hands or locking your fingers together

Any posture that hides your hands sends a signal that you're unhappy, uncomfortable, and possibly even dishonest. When it comes to hands, the key to winning people over is to keep your hands between your hips and shoulders and visible at all times.

Barbara Longsworth

▶ *Sticking your hands in your pockets.* This can be the most harmful pose when it comes to winning people over, because your hands are completely hidden. On top of that, if you jam your hands into your pockets, you may fiddle with something, which distracts people. Again, in normal situations, putting your hands in your pockets is perfectly acceptable. It sends a signal that you're at ease and confident. In tough situations, the signals are all negative: you're uninterested, evasive, deceptive, or even angry.

▶ *Holding your hands clasped behind your back.* In training, my firm refers to this as the executioner's stance, because in medieval times, guards would tie the hands of prisoners on their way to the gallows behind them. Those under arrest today often have their hands cuffed behind their backs. These are not the nonverbal signals you want to send. In addition to guilt, hands behind your back communicates the opposite of dedication and commitment.

▶ *Clasping your hands below your beltline.* We call this the fig leaf position. Although your hands are visible, the nonverbal message you're sending is, essentially, "Back off. I won't hurt you if you don't hurt me."

▶ *Crossing your arms.* This can be the most difficult stance to avoid, because it's so common in the course of normal communication. Unfortunately, it sends all kinds of negative nonverbal cues. At least one of your hands will be hidden, and perhaps both. You come across as rigid and distant because you have placed what amounts to a physical barrier between you and your audience (more on that later in this chapter). And for some reason, I've noticed, many people tend to turn away from their audience when their arms are crossed, which will be interpreted as evasive. You should square your shoulders and face your audience straight on.

▶ *Clasping your hands behind your head.* I refer to this as the "I know better than you" pose. In tough situations, when every nonverbal cue is seen in the most negative light, this position sends a signal of superiority (though in normal situations, it sends a different signal: confidence). Interestingly, the panelist who received the harshest treatment during Dr. Pierce's interview spent much of the time with his hands clasped behind his head.

▶ *Putting your hands on your hips.* When people are angry, worried, and suspicious, they will interpret this gesture as a sign of superiority—plus anger. Placing hands on hips also makes it harder to show people the palms of your hands.

▶ *Wringing your hands or locking your fingers together.* These gestures are generally perceived as aggressive, and in some cases as a lack of confidence, and therefore as a lack of expertise. This is why you need to hold your hands apart and in front of your body.

The techniques associated with the proper use of your hands remain the same whether you're standing up or sitting down, even as the mistakes you're likely to make tend to differ. While it's less likely that you'll put your hands in your pockets or adopt the executioner's stance when you're sitting, it's more likely that you'll cross your arms or clasp them behind your head. In either case, avoid putting a barrier—a lectern or a desk, for example—between you and your audience. And like Dr. Pierce, keep your hands in view and show your palms as often as possible.

The Perils of Scratching, Blinking, Licking, and Smiling

The average person can form hundreds of different facial expressions, many of which last for less than a second, and all of which convey one of the six universal emotions identified in 1972 by American psychologist Dr. Paul Ekman: anger, contempt/disgust, fear, joy/happiness, sadness, and surprise (see Figure 6.3). Ekman later expanded his list to include 11 more emotions, but we'll stick to the original six here. If you'd like to dive deeper into this fascinating subject, I included the third edition of Ekman's *Emotion in the Human Face* in the list of recommended readings at the end of this book.

FIGURE 6.3 The Six Universal Facial Expressions (You Need to Avoid)

Joy   Anger   Sadness

Disgust   Fear   Surprise

Facial-expression expert Dr. Paul Ekman has found that humans display and recognize these six universal facial expressions. One key to breaking through and winning people over is to avoid all six and maintain as neutral a facial expression as possible.

Barbara Longsworth

Whether fleeting or universal, every facial expression sends a message. Since people who are angry, worried, and suspicious interpret every message you send in the most negative light, your goal is to limit your facial expressions to those that convey caring, openness, and dedication. That can be very hard to do, and we train many of our clients to simply maintain as neutral an expression as possible. A furrowed brow, which may come across as caring or dedicated to some, may come across as skepticism or even disdain to others.

But mostly, we work with our clients to avoid four very big pitfalls when it comes to facial expression in tough situations. If you maintain as neutral a countenance as possible and avoid these pitfalls, you'll bolster your CODE score.

Touching

Numerous studies have shown that when most of us lie, our brains release chemicals known as catecholamines. Among many other physiological effects, these chemicals cause mucous membranes inside the nose and mouth to swell. This in turn causes nerve endings in the face to tingle. In simple terms, catecholamines make us itch. And when we itch, we scratch. Some call this the mucous membrane syndrome or the Pinocchio effect.

Most people aren't aware of the science behind catecholamines. Subconsciously, though, they understand and recognize the effects these chemicals cause. As we've learned, people interpret the same nonverbal signal either positively or negatively depending on the situation. The same is true here, because lying isn't the only reason your brain might release catecholamines. It can also happen when you're nervous. If you scratch an itch in the course of normal conversation, for whatever reason, no big deal. People probably won't even notice, or if they do, they'll subconsciously assume that you're nervous. In a tough situation, when every signal is interpreted in the most negative way possible, they'll think you're lying. So no matter how much your nose may itch in a difficult situation, don't scratch it. The best way to avoid the itch is to prepare, prepare, prepare. If you're not nervous, and assuming you're not lying, you're less likely to fall victim to the mucous membrane syndrome.

Blinking

Experts have found that the rate at which most people blink is closely connected to whether they are experiencing pleasant or unpleasant feelings. Joseph Tecce, Ph.D., a body language expert at Boston College, argues that while blink rate does not necessarily correlate with lying (though other experts believe it does), it definitely influences perception in a negative way. For example, Tecce has found that in every presidential contest from 1980 to 2008 (except 2000, when George W. Bush lost the popular vote but won the presidency), the candidate with the fastest blink rate during the presidential debates went on to lose the election. Barack Obama broke the streak in 2012, when he defeated Mitt Romney despite blinking much faster during their first debate. See Figure 6.4 for another presidential example in support of the idea that people draw negative conclusions from rapid blinking.

Again, preparation is the best defense against excessive blinking. Keep in mind that *too little* blinking also can undermine your CODE score. Blink too little, and you'll look like a robot and risk offending people who don't like to be stared or glared at.

FIGURE 6.4 President Clinton's Press Conference "Tell"

Facial cues can have a huge effect on the perception of trust and cred-ibility. The average person blinks at a rate of between 15 and 25 times per minute. One of the highest blink rates—120 times per minute, or roughly six times the average rate—belongs to President Bill Clinton. He blinked at that rate when he held a news conference to deny that he had had any sexual relationship with Monica Lewinsky. He also touched his nose 26 times. These nonverbal signals strongly suggested that the president was nervous and uncomfortable. Many experts, including Dr. Paul Ekman, a pioneer in the study of emotions and facial expressions, have claimed they knew the president was lying when they watched his news conference.

Wikipedia, public domain

Licking Lips

The same physiological response that can cause your nose to itch also can lead you to lick your lips. Again, in a normal situation, no one would hold this against you. In a tough situation, audiences will perceive this to mean that you're uncomfortable and dishonest. A good way to guard against all the problems that catecholamines can cause is to drink a little water before you head into a tough situation, to help keep your mucous membranes moist. Just don't drink too much. You don't want to be fidgety because you need to use the bathroom. A little clear lip balm can help as well.

Smiling

In the early days of risk communication, experts often recommended self-deprecating humor as a way to demonstrate humility and boost your CODE score. Over the years, however, new research has shown that any type of humor—even jokes you aim at yourself—is often perceived in a negative way. Angry, worried, and suspicious people don't want to think you find their concerns amusing. That means you're not taking them seriously, which will cause you to lose caring and dedication points. Today, my firm counsels clients to not even smile unless they're absolutely sure it won't affect their CODE score. That can be hard, especially when someone throws a strange or weird question at you.

During training, my firm often shows a video clip of an official from the Social Security Administration (SSA). He's appearing on the ABC program *20/20* to defend the agency's decision to deny disability benefits to a blind woman suffering from multiple sclerosis. He starts off well and even successfully expresses a little caring and empathy. Then the reporter asks what would seem to be a simple question: What is the definition of "substantial work," which is the measure by which the SSA determines whether someone qualifies for benefits? Basically, if someone is capable of doing substantial work, that person is not eligible for benefits. Unfortunately, the SSA representative doesn't know the answer, and he starts to make every mistake in the book. He leans back. His eyes dart from left to right and up and down. He crosses his arms. Finally, he looks back at the reporter, a big smile breaks out on his face, and he says, "I don't know what the definition of substantial work is."

The people to whom we show this clip typically watch quietly while the SSA representative self-destructs. When he smiles, the room erupts in moans and groans. Of all the mistakes he makes, the smile does the most damage.

STANDING FIRM, FORWARD, AND FRIENDLY

When it comes to how you stand or sit, the key to breaking through and winning people over is really the same as it is for the eyes and hands: you must send signals that show you're caring, open, and dedicated.

Most importantly, your feet should be still. If you're standing up in front of an audience, plant both feet firmly on the floor—unless, of course, you're moving around a stage or a room (which is OK, as long as you don't move too quickly and distract people). In tough situations, people will interpret "nervous feet" as a sign that you're uncomfortable, at best, or lying, at worst.

When you're sitting, an open posture is best. Sit on the edge of the chair, and lean in toward your audience (or, in the case of a media interview, toward the reporter), though not so far forward that you invade the audience's or reporter's personal space. Many men, myself included, like to rest one foot or ankle on the other knee. That's all right, as long as you continue to lean forward. Crossing one leg over another or wrapping one foot around the other, as women tend to do, also is acceptable. In both cases, remember not to cross your arms. That immediately turns an open posture into a closed one. Also, keep in mind the rules for the proper use of hands in a sitting position, as we described for Dr. Pierce. If the chair has arms, rest your elbows on them and hold your hands in front of you. Try to avoid clasping them together; I prefer to touch my fingertips together. And as described earlier in the chapter, show your open hands to the audience as often as possible, especially when you're speaking.

Whether you're standing or sitting, keep your hips and shoulders square, and face your audience. If you're addressing an individual in a group—responding to a question, for example—step slightly toward the person, and square yourself to her. When you're done, step back, and square yourself to the center of the room again. No matter the situation, you should always be leaning slightly toward your audience—again, without invading anyone's personal space. Even when standing, you can bend a little at the hips or rest on the balls of your feet. By leaning in, you signal to audience members that you're interested in and care about what they have to say, and that you welcome their thoughts and questions.

The head is the last stop on our tour of proper body posture, and the same basic rules apply. Keep your head still and level. If you tilt your head too far back, you'll appear superior and aloof. Too far forward, and you'll look, well, a little creepy. Perhaps the toughest trap to avoid when it comes to head posture is nodding or shaking your head when someone is speaking to you, particularly when you're listening to comments or questions. In tough situations, people are likely to make accusations when they speak. In training, many of my clients tend to nod along during an accusation, as if they're trying to say, "I understand" or "I hear you." That's understandable, but that's not the nonverbal message they're sending. Instead, they're saying, "The accusation you're making is true." Other clients do the opposite: they shake their heads to suggest they disagree with the accusation. Also understandable, but that's not the message that will be received. Instead, the audience will interpret a head shake as a sign that you're dismissing the accusation—and the underlying concern—as unworthy or irrelevant.

As with so many other techniques involved in winning people over, the best way to become comfortable with body posture is to practice in front of a mirror, so you can judge for yourself what nonverbal signals you're sending and fix any problems. That may seem awkward, but remember that effective communication in a tough situation is a performance. Actors and dancers (as well as TV anchormen, like my brother) spend hours and hours staring at themselves in the mirror. They understand that for any skill, practice makes perfect. And if you've perfected the ideas described in this chapter, you can still keep learning more sophisticated techniques like the ones Oprah Winfrey uses (see Figure 6.5).

DRESSING FOR SUCCESS

When it comes to clothing, the rule of thumb for boosting your CODE score is to avoid anything that might distract people from what you're saying. Men should avoid ties or shirts with crazy patterns, for example, while women should avoid gaudy jewelry, low-cut blouses, and short skirts. Simple patterns and solid colors work best (for television, too).

In one-on-one situations, common sense prevails. If you're disciplining an employee or fighting it out with your significant other, chances are you'll be dressed appropriately. In front of large groups, dress one level above what you expect the best-dressed person in your audience to wear. This allows you to earn CODE points for caring and expertise without appearing condescending or superior.

Remember the example in Chapter 4 of a New York company charged with cleaning up an old contaminated site? The state agency that regulated the company called a public meeting at the local high school (a lot of these difficult meetings seem to occur at high schools). We knew most people would be dressed casually, some in jeans and others in slacks. So we counseled our client team to wear sports coats. The regulator, who didn't ask our advice, wore a tie. The contrast was striking. He made plenty of other mistakes—standing behind a lectern, tossing out lots of jargon—but the way he dressed only made things worse. While our clients escaped the meeting largely unscathed, the

FIGURE 6.5 Wending Like Oprah

The most highly skilled credibility communicators don't just send nonverbal signals; they receive them as well. If you're on top of your game and sense that you've established trust and credibility with a large audience, one advanced technique involves physically moving into the audience—in effect, becoming one of them. At this level, you've removed the final barrier: space itself. I call this the Oprah technique, because Oprah Winfrey used it so effectively during the early days of her successful talk show (though, in her case, the situation wasn't difficult or hostile). If you engage in this technique, don't forget to continue to monitor your audience's signals. If you sense that your credibility is under attack or eroding, slowly disengage and step away from the audience. Remember, this is an advanced tactic that can backfire quickly if not done properly. *©iStockphoto.com/EdStock*

Q&A with the regulator got pretty heated, almost to the point where we had to call security.

Here are my general rules for dress if you're a man, and since I'm no fashion guru I'll ask female readers to take their cues for how to dress in tough situations:

▶ If your audience will be wearing shorts and T-shirts, wear jeans and a collared shirt.

▶ If your audience will be wearing jeans, wear slacks and a buttoned-down shirt.

▶ If your audience will be wearing slacks, wear a jacket and tie.

▶ If your audience will be wearing jackets and ties, wear a suit.

And if your audience is wearing suits, well, that's as high as you need to go. I've never run across a situation where I've recommended that a client wear a tuxedo or ball gown.

ARRIVAL AND DEPARTURE

If you're about to enter a tough situation, one where your audience is going to be angry, worried, and suspicious of everything you say, chances are your instinct will be to show up at the last minute. Then when you're done, you'll want to hightail it out of there as quickly as possible. That's perfectly natural. Why would you want to expose yourself to criticism and difficult questions any longer than necessary? To put it simply, you want to because you want to score CODE points, and arriving late and leaving early send all the wrong nonverbal messages.

Remember what we learned about Mr. Malone in Chapter 5. When it comes to arrival and departure, win people over by arriving early and staying late. When you arrive, take the chance to introduce yourself to people one-on-one or in small groups. You might be able to answer some of the toughest questions—and defuse some people's anger and suspicion—before the meeting even begins. These encounters will also provide you with anecdotes you can use later if you take questions from the audience: "You know, your neighbor Steve asked me the same question before the meeting began. Let me tell you what I told him . . ."

If possible, be the last one to leave the room. When the formal session ends, announce that you're willing to stay as long as it takes to answer any "quiet questions" that people have. Chances are some people will come up to you afterward. Most will leave, but even those who do may look over their shoulders as they walk out the door and see you standing there, living up to your promise. You'll earn big dedication and commitment points. Like Mr. Malone, you should also provide contact information or give out the address of a website that provides additional information, so people can follow up with you after the meeting is over.

REMEMBER, BARRIERS CREATE . . . BARRIERS

The earlier discussion about how to talk with your hands mentioned that crossing your arms in front of you is a definite don't. That's mainly because this stance creates a physical barrier between you and your audience (and also hides at least one of your hands).

Barriers send the wrong nonverbal signals in difficult situations. Crossing your arms sends signals of discomfort and superiority: "I'm not one of you, I know better than you, and I don't want you getting too close." Physical barriers such as desks, tables, and lecterns do the same (see Figure 6.6). They separate you from your audience, when your goal is to score CODE points by becoming accepted, liked, and believed.

FIGURE 6.6 Don't Let a Lectern Get in Your Way

As commander of coalition forces during the Gulf War, Gen. Norman Schwarzkopf proved himself to be a natural at credibility communication. He used every technique to its full advantage, as here when he stepped out from behind his lectern, removing the barrier, during a press briefing.

AP Images

Barriers also often become crutches. Most people who stand behind a lectern tend to lean on it or hold it, hiding their hands and often creating a distraction (tapping on the side, or banging for emphasis).

We've discussed techniques for scoring CODE points when you're forced to sit behind a table. But the best solution to barriers is to get rid of them. If you call an employee into your office for a difficult conversation, move your chair out from behind your desk and sit right across from the employee. When you speak in front of a large group, ask for a lavalier microphone (one that clips to your tie or jacket) so you can get out from behind a lectern or table and speak directly to the audience.

All of these techniques for nonverbal communication are important for breaking through and winning people over in tough situations, whether you're a man or a woman. But as the next chapter explains, there are some differences in how women and men earn credibility.

Chapter 7

THE CREDIBILITY GENDER GAP

The difference between men and women is that, if given the choice between saving the life of an infant or catching a fly ball, a woman will automatically choose to save the infant, without even considering if there's a man on base.

—DAVE BARRY,
AUTHOR AND COLUMNIST

Americans hold many biases when it comes to judging credibility. Research shows that when it comes to breaking through and winning people over in tough situations, one of the most important biases is gender.

Before you have a chance to say anything, angry, worried, and suspicious people begin to assess whether you are a trustworthy and credible person, based in part on whether you are a man or a woman. They can't help it. Perceptions of the roles that men and women play in society have been instilled in us by thousands of years of cultural traditions and beliefs.

Once again, perception is the key word. Remember the very first equation we discussed in Chapter 2: perception equals reality. When you're faced with a hostile audience in a tough situation, you have to set aside your own reality when it comes to gender roles. You're operating, as always, on the perception side of that equation.

How Your Gender Affects Your CODE Score

Gender affects an audience's take on every element of your CODE score: caring, openness, dedication, and expertise. So let's review each criterion in turn.

Caring

When I train people in the strategies, skills, and techniques necessary to break through and win people over, I ask participants to raise their hands if they think that, in general, women are more caring than men. Almost every hand in the room goes up. Then I ask how many think men are more caring than women. I have yet to see a serious hand go up (occasionally one guy will throw up his hand just to get a laugh).

My personal mini polls support the broader academic research. The vast majority of Americans, both men and women, believe that women are more caring than men, simply by virtue of their gender. Women take care of people. They work as nurses and teachers. They worry about other people's feelings as well as their own. In contrast, men are callous and closed off. They're selfish. They don't talk about their feelings—or so most people think. Society reinforces these biases. When was the last time you saw a television sitcom where the mother is a bungling oaf and the father is the caring, soothing voice of reason?

We all know that plenty of men are very caring; I like to think of myself that way. Certainly I've known women who aren't. Plenty of men are nurses and teachers. But the overwhelming perception is that the average woman is far more caring than the average man. As we learned in Chapter 5, caring accounts for 50 percent of your CODE score, so this is a very important truth. Again, set aside your personal biases. You're operating on the perception side of the equation, and most people—both men and women—in a tough situation will automatically assume a woman is more caring than a man.

Later on, in Chapter 10, we're going to review a model for structuring responses to the most difficult questions that angry, worried, and suspicious people ask in tough situations. The first part of that response involves expressing caring and empathy. Now you know why men have to spend more time doing that than women.

Openness

Most Americans—again, both men and woman—consider women to be more open than men. Women like to talk about their feelings. They tell their friends everything. Men only want to talk about sports, if they want to talk at all. When I conduct my mini polls and ask which gender my clients believe to be more open, almost every hand goes up to vote for women. Only a few people raise their hands in favor of men.

This means that if you're a man walking into a tough situation, your audience will be more likely to believe that you're willing to lie to them—or at least to mislead them. It takes extra effort for men to boost the openness portion of their CODE scores, because it starts at a much lower level to begin with.

It's not that women can't lose openness points; the mere fact of their gender only gets women so far. During our training sessions, we often show a clip from an old segment that aired on ABC's *20/20* program. The story is about usury, or charging unreasonably and even illegally high interest rates on credit card balances. One of the banks featured in the story—not one of my firm's clients—was smart enough to provide a female spokesperson for an interview. Unfortunately, she made almost every mistake in the book. She looked guilty and scared, because her eyes darted from side to side and up and down. Most importantly, when asked a very simple question, she gave an evasive, confusing answer. When the reporter asked the question again, she contradicted herself and then finally said she didn't know the answer. Her CODE score plummeted, and she failed to break through and win anyone over.

Dedication

Who wakes up, feeds the kids, takes them to school, goes to work, picks up the kids, drives them to after-school activities, cooks dinner, cleans up, helps with homework, puts the kids to the bed, and then prepares everything for the next day—Mom or Dad? Meanwhile, who comes home, collapses into a chair in the family room with a beer, and watches the ball game?

Most of us realize that that's not the reality in many American homes these days, including mine. I'm a single dad of two wonderful but, let's face it, demanding kids. That list of activities in the previous paragraph describes one of my typical days.

But because I'm a man, most Americans assume I lack dedication. To win people over, I have to *convince* people that I'm dedicated—not to mention caring and open.

It's important to note that people don't subtract and add gender-based CODE points consciously; they mostly do it without thinking about it. And since I'm writing this book during an election year, I'll point out that perceptions of trust and credibility based on gender drive presidential campaigns as well. Now you know why candidates trot out their families every chance they get, and even why they kiss the proverbial babies. Since every major-party presidential nominee has been a man, the candidates have had to show Americans that they're caring, open, and dedicated.

Expertise

By this point in the mini-poll portion of my training sessions, the men are starting to get a little depressed. They've learned that no matter what they may be like in real life, people who don't know them will assume that they're uncaring, closed off, and selfish in tough situations. So I throw them a bone, in the form of the fourth CODE criterion: expertise. Finally, we've come to a category in which men prevail! Ask Americans whether men or women are more expert at their jobs, and most Americans will choose men. As with the other criteria, this is true whether you ask men or women.

And the Winner Is . . .

As Figure 7.1 shows, a woman walks into a tough situation with a CODE score of 80. As we discussed, that doesn't mean a

FIGURE 7.1 Gender and the CODE Score for Credibility

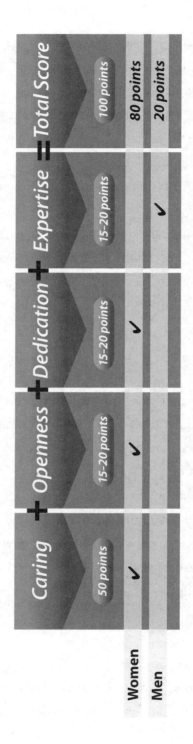

This figure demonstrates how women dominate men when it comes to the CODE score. The check marks indicate which gender walks into a tough situation with a head start for each criterion.

Barbara Longsworth

woman's credibility can't erode if she makes mistakes, but most angry, worried, and suspicious people will find a woman to be more trustworthy and credible simply by virtue of her gender. A man, in contrast, enters the same situation with a CODE score of only 20—and with a much steeper hill to climb. It should come as no surprise then that when my firm works with clients who need to break through and win people over in tough situations, we counsel them to send a woman.

When I discuss the credibility gender gap in training sessions, someone invariably asks me a version of the following question: "Let's say the audience is a group of angry, male auto mechanics. Wouldn't it make more sense to send a male mechanic to talk to them?"

I answer by telling the audience to remember that both men and women perceive women to be more caring, open, and dedicated, and men to be more expert. Even if she's facing a room full of suspicious men, a female auto mechanic still walks onto the stage with a CODE score of 80. In a scenario like this one, she may have to work harder to earn the other 20 points for expertise, but it's still easier for a woman to convince her audience that she's an expert than for a man to convince his audience that he's caring, open, and dedicated.

GENDER BIASES ARE CHANGING

By now I hope it has become clear that one of this book's sub-themes is that you need to take into consideration society's impact on people's perceptions and attitudes and to adjust your approach based on how these perceptions and attitudes change over time.

This is particularly true when it comes to gender bias, because those perceptions and attitudes are evolving before our eyes.

Every year, more men become stay-at-home dads, and more women become doctors, lawyers, and other professionals. In fact, that describes my best friend's household exactly. And in 2008, we had our first truly credible female candidate for president. During the summer of 2010, the Supreme Court welcomed its fourth female justice, Elena Kagan. As the roles of men and women in society change, so too will people's perceptions of and attitudes toward their respective levels of trust and credibility.

I see the evolution in my own work. Fifteen years ago, when I asked clients whether men or women are more dedicated, women won overwhelmingly. When I ask the same question today, the vote still favors women—but not by as much. I remember the first training session, in September 2010, when the vote tilted a little bit toward men for the first time (granted, that particular session included a lot of men). Women in my sessions also increasingly bristle at the idea that men are perceived to be more expert simply because they are men. Women continue to dominate when it comes to caring and openness in my mini polls, but I suspect that will begin to change soon as well.

What's clearly true is that over the next 10 or 20 years, the credibility gender gap will continue to narrow. One day, it may disappear altogether. Until then, the credibility gender gap is very real and an important part of breaking through and winning people over.

TIPS FOR OVERCOMING GENDER BIASES

Women should take every opportunity to bolster the expertise portion of their CODE scores, while men need to emphasize aspects of their lives that demonstrate they are caring, open, and dedicated. The fact is you can overcome these gender biases, whatever your gender, in any situation. Here are some tips for both genders.

Tips for Men and Women

The following guidelines are important for both men and women:

▶ *Bolster your CODE scores on paper.* Look for opportunities to share your bio before you enter a tough situation (and when you're applying for a job or gunning for a promotion). Take a look at what your bio conveys in terms of credibility. Chances are it's filled with information about your accomplishments at work, degrees you've earned, and awards you've won. That's terrific if you're a woman. Women have to bolster the expertise portion of their CODE scores, so details like those make sense. Men are already assumed to be experts; they don't need to convince anyone with a long list of credentials. Instead, men need to find a way to emphasize activities that bolster the other elements of their CODE scores. Do you coach Little League? Devote time to a charity? Serve on the board of your kids' daycare center? Add those to your bio.

▶ *Take control of how you're introduced.* In tough situations where someone is going to introduce you, make sure the introduction includes information that will bolster the CODE criteria you lack because of your gender. For women, that means your years of experience, academic degrees, and awards you've won. For men, include some information about your family, hobbies, community service, and charitable activities, along with the more traditional information. Before I start any training presentation, I ask the person who introduces me to mention that I'm a single father of two who enjoys running and reading. Even though I rarely speak in tough situations (I leave that to my clients), I find that a little caring, openness, and dedication in an introduction helps to establish a bond with my audiences.

▶ *Dress for success.* As we discussed in Chapter 6, the way we dress sends a lot of signals about how caring, open, dedicated, and expert we are. Remember that both men and women should dress one level above what their audience is wearing. So if the audience will be wearing T-shirts and jeans, wear slacks and a dress shirt. If the audience will be wearing slacks and dress shirts, wear a suit. Women need to avoid gaudy jewelry, low-cut blouses, and short skirts. Men should steer away from shirts or ties with crazy patterns. In other words, eliminate anything that will distract people from what you're saying.

I wrote part of this chapter during one of the business conventions I attend every year. During a break, I sat in on a session about how organizations can tap into their grassroots and influence public policy. In Washington, D.C., we call it "advocacy." From the very beginning of the session, I felt like something was wrong. The two presenters weren't connecting with me, and I found my mind wandering. About 10 minutes in, it hit me: they were under-dressed—especially the man, who had on a short-sleeve button-down shirt, untucked, paired with dirty, wrinkled khakis. I thought to myself, "You know, it wouldn't kill him to at least wear a sports coat to show us a little respect. He's not taking this seriously." I wasn't listening to what he was saying because I was distracted by what he was wearing. This wasn't a tough situation; certainly I wasn't angry, worried, and suspicious. But I noticed what the pre-senters were wearing, and it gave me a negative feeling. I wound up leaving the session early so I could run back to my hotel room and add this anecdote to this chapter.

Tips for Women

The following tips will help women address their perceived dis-advantage in expertise:

▶ *Work in some numbers.* Research shows that people inter-pret math skills as a sign of an organized, analytical—and therefore expert—mind. Women can use this to their advantage. If you're itemizing factors or features or rea-sons, number them when speaking and writing. As I've said, my firm does a lot of work for the nuclear power industry, so I'll use that as an example here. Say you've expressed caring and empathy and want to share three rea-sons why next-generation nuclear reactors are superior to those that exist today. Do it this way: "Number one, these reactors incorporate passive safety features that work even if the plant loses power. Number two, next-generation reactors produce less waste than today's models. Number three, like all reactors, next-generation versions emit no greenhouse gases." If you're speaking in public, hold up one, two, and then three fingers as you're listing the reasons. Men can do this, too, although it's not necessary. It certainly won't subtract from men's CODE scores.

▶ *Speak with authority.* You know you're an expert, but if you're a woman, your tone of voice and air of authority are critical in getting others to believe what you say. Candy Tymson, an Australian expert on gender communications and author of the 2003 book *Gender Games: Doing Business with the Opposite Sex*, advises her female clients to "speak up . . . and stand up for yourself," especially when communicating with men. With our clients, my firm recommends that women lower the pitch of their voices slightly and avoid sounding deferential or self-effacing. We also encourage women to avoid discussing anything that may be perceived as overly personal; women don't need the caring, openness, and dedication points, and getting too personal can make it harder to earn those last 20 expertise points. Communications expert Rosalind Sedacca also advises women to "avoid raising your voice in a questioning tone at the end of sentences. When your voice goes up, your credibility goes down."

▶ *Suppress the urge to smile.* Remember that the research on the use of humor in tough situations has evolved, and my firm now counsels our clients not even to smile. While this applies equally to men and women, women tend to smile more often. They also respond more positively to people who smile at them, which means they're more likely to smile back. It's an urge that women especially have to resist.

A Tip for Men

Although men are at a disadvantage on three criteria, this single tip can help them address all three perceived weaknesses:

▶ *Speak with feeling.* Men can show caring through the way they present themselves and what they discuss. In tough situations, a man must find ways to connect emotionally, such as mentioning his wife and kids, his experience in the community, or something that touched him about the topic or issue he's discussing. Remember all the things Mr. Malone did right in Chapter 5. It's also essential that men show they are caring, open, and dedicated by expressing empathy with the concerns of their audiences.

GENDER ISN'T THE WHOLE STORY

Let me close with one last anecdote. One of my firm's clients recently came under attack from critics who questioned the way the company did business. National Public Radio (NPR) decided to devote an hour to the story and invited our client to participate in an interview. Because NPR planned to have two critics on the program, we offered two spokespeople of our own: one man and one woman. Going in, I was a little worried about the man, because both critics were women, and this was definitely a tough situation. Plus the NPR program was a call-in show, and I knew plenty of angry, worried, and suspicious people would call in.

As it turned out, both of our spokespeople did great. If anything, the man came across as more caring and open, and the woman nudged him slightly on expertise. They made quite a team. It's a reminder that with practice and preparation, both men and women can break through and win people over in tough situations (although, all other things being equal, if you have a choice, send a woman).

Tough situations include potentially hostile media interviews. In the next chapter, I'll share what we've learned that can help you succeed if you ever find yourself in front of a camera or confronted by a newspaper reporter.

Chapter 8

MASTERING THE MEDIA

It's amazing that the amount of news that happens in the world every day always just exactly fits the newspaper.

—Jerry Seinfeld, comedian

Many years ago, I escorted a client, let's call her Ms. Goble, to a local television station. The station asked her to come in for an interview on a controversial education issue, and we expected she would face some fairly difficult, hostile questions. I had prepared her well in terms of what she needed to convey both verbally and nonverbally. She had lots of stories about the kids her organization had helped. Her messages were well tested and finely honed.

What I hadn't prepared her for quite so well was the chaos she encountered or the mechanics of the interview itself. Television studios are crazy places. People are running everywhere. Phones are ringing. Bright, hot lights go on and off. In this particular case, the station set up Ms. Goble for a live-remote (the kind of interview we discussed briefly in Chapter 6). Even though she was in the studio, she wasn't going to speak to the reporter face-to-face. She would be talking into a camera while listening to the reporter's questions through what's called an IFB (for "interruptible feedback") stuck in her ear. They set her up in the newsroom, so people were working behind her and in front of her. Ms. Goble was a fairly seasoned media performer, but she had never faced this particular setup, and it rattled her a little.

In the end, she did just fine. She knocked every question out of the park and sent all the right nonverbal signals. We were both very pleased with her performance. But as we left the station, I promised myself that I would never fail a client that way again. In this chapter, we're going to conduct some basic media training. Breaking through and winning people over in tough situations is hard enough. When you're also facing a camera or a recorder or even a print reporter with a pencil and steno book, the strategies, skills, and techniques you need to use with people when they're angry, worried, and suspicious of everything you say become even more important.

THE MEDIA REVOLUTION

I opened this book with an account of how the media handled presidential affairs that occurred 35 years apart. In the early 1960s, they didn't cover President Kennedy's indiscretions at all. In the late 1990s, they couldn't stop covering President Clinton's relationship with Monica Lewinsky.

That's just one facet of a media revolution that began in the late 1960s, one that has accelerated significantly in the twenty-first century. It's a completely different business today, and anyone who conducts interviews—whether in normal or tough situations—has had to adjust to an environment that's faster, rougher, and more intense than ever. Volumes have been written about this ongoing revolution, but let me highlight some of the changes that have most significantly affected how my firm and our clients interact with the media from a practical standpoint.

The 24-Hour News Cycle

In 1980, CNN introduced the 24-hour news cycle. Before CNN, people generally had to wait until the evening news to hear about stories that had happened during the day, and they had to wait for the morning news shows and newspapers to learn about news that broke overnight. (If it was a really significant story, however, the broadcast networks would interrupt their regular programming with special reports.) CNN made the news available around the clock for the first time, as long as you had access to a television and cable services.

In the twenty-first century, the Internet, smartphones, tablet computers, Twitter, and other technologies and platforms have made news ubiquitous and instantaneous. For our clients, the consequence is that anything that happens anywhere can draw them into a media interview with very little notice. As I'm writing this chapter, Hurricane Isaac just struck the Gulf Coast. Within hours, authorities warned that a dam in Mississippi was in danger of giving way, and the state ordered 50,000 people to evacuate. My firm had a brand-new client at the time, and they started receiving calls from the media within minutes of the announcement. But we hadn't been working with them long enough to prepare them properly to do interviews, and while they talked to a couple of reporters, we weren't able to take full advantage of a big opportunity for them to tell their story and convey their messages. Round-the-clock and omnipresent media place a huge premium on planning and preparation. The days when people and companies had hours to react to a breaking story are long gone. Now it's more like minutes.

Shorter, Simpler Stories

Gannett changed the way newspapers report the news when it launched *USA Today* in 1982. The paper presented information in easily digestible bites with shorter stories, bullet points, graphics, and color. Television news has followed suit. Broadcast stories feature lots of graphics that change constantly, which drives me crazy but appeals to the MTV and future generation.

Because of *USA Today*, the stories our clients tell and the messages they deliver in print have to be shorter and simpler, too. Remember what we discussed in Chapter 2: shoot for words and concepts that an eighth- or ninth-grader can understand. Indeed, *USA Today* influenced this book and how it presents information about winning people over. Since my goal for the book was to make it a simple, practical, and easily digestible resource, I've included plenty of bulleted lists, figures, and tables. I would have published it in color, but my publisher said no.

USA Today also contributed to another trend involving the use of ordinary people, rather than experts and officials, in stories. This is another consequence of the broader decline in how much we trust and believe people in positions of authority. Studies have shown we trust "people like us" more than any other source, so that's what the media give us.

In our media training, we often show two video clips. The first is an *ABC News* story from 1970, when President Nixon signed the Clean Air Act, a landmark piece of environmental legislation. The entire story takes place in the White House. President Nixon is the only one given a sound bite, and it lasts for more than 30 seconds. Twenty years later, President George H. W. Bush signed into law a series of important amendments to the 1970 Clean Air Act. The second clip shows an NBC report on the legislation. President Bush is nowhere to be seen. The entire piece is about how the law will affect real people out in the real world. Only two people have sound bites, both "average Americans" who like the new law because it will help people who suffer from asthma and cut back on the number of fish killed as a result of acid rain. Their sound bites last about five seconds each. That's not much time to tell a story or even to convey a message—not to mention to win people over—especially when you're competing against Kim Kardashian and Lindsay Lohan. It's just another reason, by the way, for why compelling stories are important. That's what today's media are looking for.

Corporate Media Ownership

In 1985, a company called Capital Cities Communications purchased ABC, and General Electric bought NBC. For the first time, formerly independent news operations became divisions within larger corporations. Those corporations focused more intently on the bottom line and demanded ever-greater profits. That's when information and entertainment began to fuse into "infotainment." During another round of consolidation in the mid-1990s, the Walt Disney Company bought Capital Cities/

ABC, and Westinghouse bought CBS (and then morphed into a big entertainment company called Viacom). Today, or at least as I'm writing this, three of the four major U.S. networks are owned by larger entertainment companies: Disney (ABC), NBCUniversal (NBC), and Fox (News Corporation). The fourth, CBS, became an independent news organization in 2011.

Combined with the advent of cable and other competing outlets, these consolidations drove the competition for ratings to new heights. Fareed Zakaria, a journalist who works for *Time* magazine and CNN, once described the news business in the new millennium this way: "I don't believe that television networks necessarily have a liberal bias or a conservative bias. What they all have is an 'eyeball' bias. They'll do whatever they need to do to make sure you don't change the channel."

This competition places a lot of value on personality. It also means that to tell our stories and convey our messages, we have to compete for media attention against everything from war and the economy to Tom Cruise and *Dancing with the Stars*—subjects that on the surface may seem to be much more compelling for viewers and readers, and therefore more attractive to the media.

Immediacy Goes Global

In 1987, CNN launched Newsource, a satellite-based communications service that allows television stations to upload and download video from and to virtually anywhere in the world. When news happens anywhere, the television stations in your hometown can air video almost immediately. After creating the 24-hour news cycle, CNN stretched it globally.

For our clients with global interests, or interests here at home that may be affected by what happens in other countries, that means being ready to address problems that may occur anywhere on the planet. The competition to get the story first is red-hot, and reporters need expert, compelling—not to mention trustworthy and credible—sources almost immediately when news breaks. If you hope to be part of a story, or if you need to respond to a crisis, time is of the essence. Again, that requires planning and preparation. Rather than hours or even days, you may have only minutes to engage.

Online News Coverage

Finally, in the single most disruptive change to the media landscape during the past 50 years, the general public gained access to the Internet in 1991. The World Wide Web has remade completely the way news is gathered, reported, and consumed. According to a 2012 survey by the Pew Research Center's Project for Excellence in Journalism, more than half of all Americans now get at least some of their news online.

While this topic warrants an entirely separate book, let me make a few points that will help to put the Internet's impact on the media in perspective:

▶ Without the *Drudge Report*, the online news aggregation site, it's possible that no one ever would have heard the name Monica Lewinsky. Arguably the most consequential story of the 1990s might never have been told.

▶ You may remember that in 2002, Mississippi's Republican senator Trent Lott made some insensitive racial remarks at a 100th birthday party for his South Carolina colleague and fellow Republican, Strom Thurmond. The remarks generated one small traditional story by *ABC News* reporter Ed O'Keefe in early December, and then nothing. But several prominent bloggers kept the story alive online, and they pounded away relentlessly at the traditional media for not making a bigger deal out of what they considered to be a major story. The embers they nurtured eventually engulfed Lott in a major media firestorm, and on December 20, just a little more than two weeks after he made the remarks, Lott resigned as Senate Majority Leader. This represented the first time that the blogosphere, or non-traditional media, drove coverage of such an important story. It has happened many times since (see Figure 8.1 for another example).

▶ Newspapers are migrating online. I still read the newspaper that arrives on my doorstep each morning, in part because my father was in the newspaper business his whole career, and I'm not a big fan of change. But I'm one of a dwindling number of print subscribers. By the time I pull the bag off the paper and snap open the front page, the news it contains is at least 12 hours old. If I want the latest information, I go online. Not long ago, we counseled clients that one advantage to print interviews was longer lead time and more room to tell their stories. That's not so much the case anymore, as print reporters vie with their broadcast competitors to be first. Lesley Stahl, the veteran CBS correspondent, has bemoaned this trend, arguing that the pressure to say something—anything!—is so great that

FIGURE 8.1 Tsunami by Way of Cell Phone

The story of the 2004 Indian Ocean tsunami unfolded not through traditional coverage by mainstream news outlets but in messages from the people directly affected by the disaster. Using their cell phones, they sent texts, e-mails, photos, and video clips to the outside world from remote locations that traditional journalists couldn't reach. As massive cost cutting, driven by competition, has led to fewer reporters and bureaus, the advent of handheld communications technology has led the mainstream media to rely increasingly on "citizen journalists" to supplement—and, in some cases, drive—their news coverage.

©iStockphoto.com/Mari

reporters increasingly share information that they haven't fully vetted. When Stahl appeared on a History Channel documentary on journalism that aired in 2000, she said:

"This 24-hour business puts so much pressure on journalists . . . it's frightening, because when you're out there as a reporter and [producers] are pressuring you to just fill three minutes or five minutes, you'll start putting on rumors. You're desperate."

▶ It's often little more than rumor and innuendo. That cuts both ways for our clients. Online outlets provide more opportunities to tell stories and convey messages, but they contribute to the trend toward ever-narrowing bands of audiences. They also get things wrong more often, because they usually operate without the editors and fact-checkers that traditional news outlets employ. And if you don't have an immediate comment, they'll go with the story anyway, using someone else's stories and messages.

▶ Armed with smartphones, we're all journalists now. Almost everything of significance, and plenty of stuff that isn't, is recorded by someone. As I write this chapter, England's Prince Harry is the subject of a media firestorm involving what the press is calling "naked cavorting" in a Las Vegas hotel room. Ten years ago, it's unlikely that anyone would ever have known, because no one at the party would have had a way to document and prove that it happened.

I could go on and on, but hopefully this gives you a sense of the atmosphere in which sources operate. It's impossible to predict where the revolution will take us next. One strong candidate is increasing diffusion through social media. The Pew survey found that while many journalists have taken to social-media platforms to gather and report news, only 9 percent of Americans use them to find and absorb it. Other studies suggest that while this number may be low, it's growing quickly.

Twitter especially has had a big effect on how reporters do their jobs. Even elite journalists are now more focused on getting the word out fast, in 140-character packages, than on any real analysis or in-depth reporting. All the credit goes to whoever tweets first, whether it's news of Osama bin Laden's death, Mitt Romney's vice presidential nominee, or Lindsay Lohan's latest arrest. It creates even more pressure for speed over thoughtfulness or thoroughness. You may have a shot at influencing a story *right now*, but the chance may be gone forever in only a few hours. And you'd better boil your comment down to something very short and fast—as well as entertaining and compelling.

Implications for Winning People Over

If you're like me, you find all of the change in media coverage fascinating, but adapting to these changes is what's important when it comes to winning people over. The most important rule to keep in mind when you're about to engage with the media is that everything we've discussed to this point still matters, only more so. Your objective remains the same: to establish and maintain trust and credibility. But reaching your objective can be much harder. Because of the global 24-hour news cycle, you may be thrust into a media interview at a moment's notice with little or no time to prepare.

Also, if you are interviewed, your audience undoubtedly will be much larger than a high school auditorium full of people. If a story appears in a regional newspaper, tens of thousands will read it. If you appear on *60 Minutes* (and please don't unless you spend a lot of time preparing with a consultant like me), millions will see you. Cameras and microphones make most people nervous, and so you have to monitor your nonverbal messages even more closely. Seasoned journalists ask the most difficult questions, and they are increasingly unwilling to accept talking-point answers.

Finally, if the media come calling, you are always "on." It doesn't matter where you are or whether you see a reporter or camera. You need to act and speak as if a microphone is capturing your every word and a camera is recording your every move. We used to counsel clients not to say anything they wouldn't want to read in the newspaper the next morning. Now it might be more appropriate to tell them to avoid saying anything they wouldn't want someone to tweet in the next five minutes.

Not all media interviews are hostile, of course, but you should bring all of your strategies, skills, and techniques to bear every time. They'll improve your performance, even if the interview is perfectly pleasant and normal. Plus, you never know when an interview will become hostile.

So you don't get rattled like Ms. Goble, keep these additional tips in mind as well.

Prepare with an Expert

Work with your organization's communications specialists. If you receive a call or an interview request from a reporter, get in touch with your company's public relations or communications department. Chances are your company's policy requires it anyway, and professionals can be very helpful. They probably know the reporter, or at least her reputation, and can help figure out what she's trying to learn and any angle she may have. They can also help to prepare you for an interview, because they'll remind you of the key messages that your organization will want you to convey, have a good idea of the kinds of questions you can expect, fill you in on any experience with the reporter, and hone the stories you want to tell.

If you don't work for a large company with a media relations professional, it would be worth the time and money to find a consultant who knows your issues. Engage the consultant for at least a couple of hours, to refresh you on technique and messages.

Know Your "Rights" and Your Goal

Many of my firm's clients initially assume that reporters control everything about an interview, but that's not true. You do have some say, beginning with the decision whether or not to be interviewed in the first place. We almost always counsel clients to accept, because any interview, even one that may be difficult and hostile, is an opportunity for them to tell their stories and convey their messages.

You should also ask the reporter (or producer) some questions:

▶ Why does the reporter want to interview you?
▶ How is your interview going to be used? On what platforms?
▶ What is the nature of the story?
▶ Is the reporter interviewing anyone else, and who are those people? (This can help reveal the angle the reporter plans to take.)

▶ Can you see the questions in advance?

▶ Will the reporter let you review the story before it's published or aired?

Not all reporters will answer these questions, but it doesn't hurt to ask. The answers you do get will help you decide whether or not to do the interview and—assuming you have time—figure out what you need to do to prepare.

If possible, research the reporter, too. A quick Internet search will reveal any previous coverage of the topic you're being asked to discuss and any angle or bias the reporter may have. This will also help you determine how much the reporter knows about that topic you're going to discuss. Chances are she'll know more than the average person but less than you. This will help you predict what questions she's going to ask.

Even if you're an expert on the issue, spend some time researching it online and on Twitter. You'll want to know about any breaking developments or expert commentary the reporter may know about that you don't.

Finally, remember that you have a goal in any media interview: to break through and win people over. A good way to prepare is to think about the three things you want the people who read, see, or hear the story to remember. Work those into your stories and messages.

Consider Your Audience

Your audience is not the reporter who's interviewing you. It's the readers, viewers, or listeners on the other end of the microphone or notebook. The number of people who saw Ms. Goble's interview was probably in the tens of thousands, but only a relative handful really mattered to her: the parents of schoolchildren who could benefit from the program she ran, and the policy-makers, both federal and local, whose support she needed to keep the program going. She tailored her stories and messages for them.

Consider, too, that each audience has a different level of experience, vocabulary, perceptions, and preconceptions. Ms. Goble knew that the parents in her audience were relatively poor and uneducated but that they were committed to creating a better life for their children. Her stories and messages were simple and spoke to that desire, and they came with a healthy dose of caring and empathy. Also remember the ban on jargon. In an interview, or whatever piece of the interview a reporter decides to use, you'll have no time to define any jargon you use or a reporter throws at you.

Be Concise and Repetitive

In any situation where you hope to break through and win people over, you need to be concise and repetitive. This advice is even more important in an interview. In most cases, particularly with a broadcast reporter, the whole interview likely will last less than 15 minutes. When the story airs, you'll be lucky if your sound bite is 15 seconds. The same kind of situation applies to print inter-views: you'll be lucky to get even one quote in the story. Report-ers will run through their tape or their notes and most likely use the first compelling quote that fits the story. If that quote doesn't include one or more of your messages, what was the point of doing the interview in the first place?

Repeating yourself over and over again, with no more than a few different words, will feel a little strange, but remember the preceding tip. The reporter may hear the same thing over and over again, but the people you're actually trying to reach will only read, hear, or see it once.

In a live interview, you can vary your responses a little, because everything you say will be seen or heard. But make sure each response includes a story or message, because repetition always makes it easier to win people over.

Make Eye Contact with the Reporter

The importance of eye contact with the reporter may be obvious when it comes to television interviews, but for all the reasons we discussed in Chapter 6, it's important whatever the medium. The only exception is the one Ms. Goble faced when we visited the television studio, what I referred to as a live-remote. When it's just you and a camera, look straight into the camera. I find that some of my clients actually prefer this setup, because they're a little uncomfortable maintaining eye contact for so long with an actual person. Others find it a little weird. As with anything, practice and preparation will make your experience much easier and less stressful.

Don't Just Answer the Questions

I'm reminded of one of my favorite scenes in the old TV show *M*A*S*H*. In a room full of reporters, Hawkeye and Trapper agitate a general by asking pointed questions about an incubator shortage. The exasperated general finally yells, "This is a press conference! The last thing I want to do is answer a lot of questions!"

Like any joke, that one has a kernel of truth. It's one of the messages we drive home to clients we prepare for media interviews. Your job is to win people over by telling compelling stories and delivering powerful messages; the questions a reporter asks you are really just opportunities to do so. Your stories and messages should address the question in some way, but a series of yeses and nos won't get the job done. The reporter isn't a teacher testing you; you're not a student. You're there to tell the people in your audience what you think they should know about your subject, in your own words, so don't let the reporter shape the entire conversation. Get your points out early and often, even if that means taking over the conversation with bridges to your messages.

That brings us to my next point . . .

Use Bridges

A bridge is a rhetorical tool that uses a question as a springboard, transitioning from the question to your stories and messages. Politicians do this all the time. Watch the next presidential news conference, and count the number of times the president actually answers the questions that reporters ask him. Even when he does, he won't spend a lot of time on the actual answer. He'll move quickly to whatever message he wants to convey.

Bridging can be an effective technique in both normal and tough situations, and like all of the skills we've covered in this book, it takes practice before you can do it well. It has to be done artfully; if you're too obvious about it, as many politicians are, you'll drive down your CODE score. For starters, make sure you know where the bridge is taking you. One of the clips we use in media training shows a *Today* show interview with a food safety expert from Johns Hopkins University. The program invited him to appear to discuss an outbreak of mad cow disease. Although no one actually contracted the disease, parents all over the country were terrified that their kids might catch it by eating tainted beef at school. The food safety expert intended to calm the parents, but Figure 8.2 tells what happened when he stepped out onto a bridge to nowhere.

David Axelrod, the Democratic strategist who won me over with a poignant story about his daughter's illness, is a master at the art of bridging. His favorite bridge is one that can work for anyone. When a reporter asks a question he doesn't want to answer, he often responds by saying, "Here's the larger point I think people really care about . . ." He acknowledges the question very briefly but then goes on to tell his story or deliver his message. Here are some other statements that can serve as effective bridges:

► To the contrary, I believe the most important point is . . .
► I think what people really want to know is . . .
► Rather than speculate, let's focus on what we know to be true.
► Let me share with you some of the things that I'm hearing from people I talk to.
► Good question, but first I'd like to emphasize . . .

FIGURE 8.2 Stay off Bridges to Nowhere

Bridging can be very effective, but make sure you know where the bridge is taking you. On the *Today* show, a food safety expert from Johns Hopkins University sought to calm parents' fears about mad cow disease. Anchor Katie Couric asked him whether the beef in school lunches was safe. He responded, "Yes, I do believe that they're safe. But let's put this in perspective. There are 5,000 cases of deaths from food-borne disease every year in the United States." Although "Let's put this in perspective" was a good bridge, he fell right off by mentioning the number of deaths— something Couric had never asked about. Rather than reassuring people who were angry and worried, he made the situation worse. Later, Couric repeated the same question. He said, "Yes, I think the beef is perfectly safe. I think the beef is safer than chicken . . . and chicken is safer than vegetables." Once again, he made parents more worried, not less.
©iStockphoto.com/monkeybusinessimages

Sometimes a bridge is as simple as denying the premise of a question. But you have to employ a bridge correctly. When Massachusetts senator John Kerry ran for president in 2004, the Democratic candidate was critical of President Bush's decision to go to war in Iraq even though he had voted to give Bush the authority to go to war in 2003. As a result, Kerry had a lot of trouble answering the following question: "Why did you vote to give President Bush the authority to go to war with Iraq?" Sometimes he said he thought the president should have the authority, but that he shouldn't have used it. Other times, he said he would have prosecuted the war more effectively. A separate vote to provide funding for the war led to his now infamous quote, "I actually did vote for [it] before I voted against it." The question tied him up in knots throughout the election. He never found an effective bridge from that difficult question to a satisfactory response, and some analysts blame his loss at least in part on his inability to come up with a satisfactory answer.

Another Democratic senator who eventually ran for president found the right bridge that year. New York senator Hillary Clinton faced the same dilemma as Kerry. Like him, she had voted to give President Bush authority to go to war with Iraq, but over time she came to oppose the war and, presumably, regretted her vote. Long before she declared her own candidacy in 2008, she appeared on ABC's *This Week with George Stephanopoulos*. Not surprisingly, the question came up. Here's how she handled it:

> *Stephanopoulos*: Senator Clinton, if you knew then what you know now about how President Bush has used that authority [to go to war in Iraq], would you vote to give it to him again?
>
> *Clinton*: George, we wouldn't have had a vote.

Clinton basically swiped the question aside and then launched into a stinging critique of the Bush administration's prosecution of the war (a bridge my firm refers to as a "deflection.") She would do the same throughout the campaign, and while she ultimately lost the 2008 Democratic nomination to Barack Obama (who hadn't been in the Senate when the war authority vote was taken), she never had the same problem with the issue as Kerry had.

One of our clients, the vice president of corporate communications for a global company, did media interviews almost every day. She took the concept of bridging very seriously. We helped her craft about 25 bridging statements that she would place on her desk any time she spoke to a reporter on the phone. As the interview progressed, she would run down the list to make sure she was bridging to good stories and messages. It's a good technique. In fact, feel free to use notes generally in interviews, as long as you're not on camera.

Anticipate the Easy Questions

Whether it's a media interview or a difficult discussion with an employee, it's easy to become fixated on the really tough questions you're most worried about answering. It's important to give some thought to the relatively easy questions, too. These soft-balls, as we call them, represent terrific opportunities to tell your stories and convey your messages. It's a shame to waste them.

One of the best-known examples of a wasted opportunity came in 1980, when Massachusetts senator Ted Kennedy challenged President Jimmy Carter for the Democratic presidential nomination. Shortly before officially announcing his decision to

run, Senator Kennedy scheduled an interview with CBS correspondent Roger Mudd. The senator expected a lot of difficult
questions involving the Chappaquiddick incident, in which a
young woman in his car drowned when he drove off a bridge; the
assassinations of his two older brothers; and rumors about his
drinking and womanizing. For those questions, Senator Kennedy
was well prepared. But when Mudd simply asked him, "Senator,
why do you want to be president?" he stumbled for an answer.
After hemming and hawing for what seemed like an eternity, he
finally mumbled something uninspiring about having a "great
belief in this country" and then listed a whole series of problems
the nation faced, without saying anything about what he might
do to solve them. From that point on, Senator Kennedy's poll
numbers began to fall, and he eventually dropped out of the race.

Polish Your Nonverbal Messages

Remember Chapter 6's rules about dress and posture. The same
rules apply when it comes to the media, especially in a televised
interview, but really in any medium. Don't wear anything that
will distract people from what you're saying—no gaudy jewelry
or short skirts for women, no crazy patterns on ties or shirts for
men. Solid colors are best.

One other tip applies to men who appear on television: don't
be afraid to use a little powder or pancake. Television lights can
be very hot, which can make you perspire even if you're not
nervous. A little makeup will prevent you from appearing shiny.

Lean forward during the interview to send the signal that
you're eager and engaged, even if you're sitting on a panel as
Dr. Pierce did in Chapter 4.

Correct Your Mistakes

We all make mistakes once in a while. If you make one in a media interview, feel free to go back and correct it. Reporters don't want errors in their stories, and unless they're trying to embarrass you, which usually isn't the case, even in hostile interviews, they'll edit or leave out your mistake. This is true even in live television interviews. Better to correct the record when you have the chance.

Also remember the rule about saying, "I don't know" if you don't. It's OK, as long as you don't do it too often and lose expertise points. Just as you would with any audience, make sure to follow up and provide the reporter with the answer. Finally, avoid using the expression "No comment." Those words have become a signal to people that you're covering up something.

Stay On, Always

We've all heard and seen people get caught saying things they never intended anyone to hear, because they didn't realize the microphone in front of them was live. A former colleague used to tell a great story about a visit that former Washington, D.C., mayor Marion Barry paid to the colleague's station when he was a television producer. The mayor came in with a couple of aides, and an intern escorted him to the station's green room, where he waited for the interview to begin. The mayor asked for some water, and when the intern brought it to him, she overheard him saying to one of his aides that he hoped the reporter wouldn't ask him about a particular issue (which unfortunately is lost to history). The intern gave the mayor his water, left the green room, and ran straight to my former colleague to tell him what she'd heard. Naturally, the reporter asked the mayor a whole series of questions about the issue he had hoped to avoid.

Years later, as Ms. Goble and I drove to that very same station for her interview, I cautioned her, "Assume someone is recording your every word from the moment you get out of my car until the moment you get back in and drive away." And today, the ubiquitous smartphone means you're actually still on even when you get in the car and drive away.

Bring Visuals

The old cliché that a picture is worth a thousand words is especially true when it comes to the media. Television reporters and producers are always looking for good video; in fact, good video sometimes determines which stories they cover and which ones they don't. Likewise, print and online reporters want interesting, compelling graphics and photos. If you can enhance the story you're telling with a good visual or two, take advantage.

My firm once trained a group of NASA scientists and engineers. Several months later, we were very gratified to see one of our trainees interviewed on ABC's *World News* about the future of commercial aviation. As she was talking about building planes out of metal that could bend and move to reduce wind resistance and turbulence, she demonstrated the concept by bending a piece of metal and then heating it with a lighter. The metal straightened right back out. The visual enhanced her story tremendously; in fact, it was really cool.

Be Positive

Remember the $S = B+$ equation: success comes from being positive. Even if you're heading into a hostile media interview, approach it in a positive, affirmative way. As we discussed in Chapter 2, a defensive posture can be self-fulfilling—and defensiveness will definitely come across during a televised interview.

Practice Makes Perfect

When we help prepare clients for media interviews, we spend a lot of time in mock scenarios. Clients conduct on-camera interviews and talk to a fake print reporter over the phone. You can do the same. Grab your smartphone and record yourself responding to questions, or, even better, ask a friend or colleague to play reporter for you. Nothing will prepare you better, especially for a television interview, than watching yourself on TV beforehand.

If you practice all these ideas, you'll be better prepared than Ms. Goble the next time you schedule a media interview. Even so, in any tough situation, including interviews, you may encounter traps that will trip you up and lower your CODE score. In the next chapter, we'll review the most common traps and how to avoid them—as well as what you can do to escape if you do fall in.

Chapter 9

AVOIDING AND ESCAPING TRAPS

When an elephant steps on a trap, no more trap.

—AFRICAN PROVERB

Unfortunately, we're not elephants. If you step in a trap when you're trying to break through and win people over, chances are pretty good that the trap is going to win.

Traps can exist when you're communicating in normal or tough situations, but when you step in one in a normal situation, your audience probably won't notice. Or they'll give you the benefit of the doubt and ignore it. In a tough situation, falling into a trap will begin to erode your CODE score, and if you don't escape quickly, you won't be able to win over people when they're angry, worried, and suspicious of everything you say.

It's easy enough to step into a trap all by yourself, but if the situation is hostile and high-profile enough, you may encounter people who deliberately set traps to ensnare you. Just as my firm helps to prepare business clients for tough situations, so do experts who work for opposition groups and other organizations that seek to thwart our clients' goals. They train activists on how to make it more difficult to win people over, in part by getting them angry, worried, and suspicious in the first place.

In Chapter 1, I mentioned a client that wanted to build a high-voltage power line. As part of our work, we helped organize a series of community meetings to engage residents who lived and businesses that operated along the line's proposed route. Most of the meetings went off without a hitch, but at a few, some attendees sought to disrupt the proceedings. Based on the tactics they used (accusing company representatives of lying, implying they cared about nothing but money, and throwing around a lot of jargon), we concluded that they must have been trained to undermine the strategies, skills, and techniques we've discussed in this book. They were trying to erode a communicator's trust and credibility rather than to bolster it.

To avoid traps, whether inadvertent or deliberate, it's important to know what they are, as well as how to escape if you do fall in. Based on my firm's experience in helping clients navigate tough situations, this chapter describes the most common traps to watch out for. Notice that we've touched on some of them in previous chapters.

THE PREPARATION TRAP

To be precise, we might call the first trap the lack-of-preparation trap. If you fall into this one, it's entirely your fault. Remember Senator Kennedy's ill-fated interview with Roger Mudd, described in Chapter 8. The senator had prepared carefully for all the difficult questions, but he wasn't ready for one of the simplest and most straightforward of them all: "Senator, why do you want to be president?"

One of the messages I've tried to drive home in this book is the absolute need to prepare and rehearse for tough situations in which you need to win over people when they're angry, worried, and suspicious. Communicating in situations like these is as much a skill as acting, dancing, or singing. No professional performer would ever step foot in front of an audience without sufficient rehearsal. And that's on top of the years of hard work it took to get them to the top of their professions in the first place. In a tough situation, you are onstage, essentially performing, whether you're talking one-on-one with a colleague or friend, speaking to an auditorium full of people, or conducting an interview with a television program that reaches millions.

Your rehearsal needs to cover the most difficult credibility questions you can possibly expect, as well as general fact questions—friendly ones and even out-of-the-box odd ones. You should have well-rehearsed answers that use stories conveying your key messages. This should prepare you for essentially any question that can come your way.

If you don't prepare, you will fail. It's as simple as that. And you can be sure that your opponents, if they exist, will be prepared. At one of the meetings in a community along the power line, opponents turned out dozens of angry, worried, and suspicious residents. To survive, our client's representative had to use every strategy, skill, and technique at his disposal.

If you fall into this trap, you'll have a very difficult time trying to climb out. So you have to avoid it. Here's how:

▶ Prepare with your organization's public relations or communications experts, if appropriate.

▶ Make sure you have your stories and messages set.

▶ Think about the questions you're likely to be asked and the answers you're going to give (more on how to structure those answers is coming in the next chapter), as well as the audience you're trying to reach. And be sure to remember the benign questions as well as the difficult and hostile ones.

▶ Grab a friend or a colleague for at least one tough practice session where you give your speech or presentation (without PowerPoint!), tell your stories, and respond to questions, both easy and hard.

This last point is the most important. You really can't over-prepare. My firm gives a lot of presentations to potential clients whose business we seek. Before we go "live," we engage in multiple dress rehearsals to make sure we're ready and the stories we want to tell and messages we want to convey are honed to a fine point. I can tell you from experience that delivering a presentation in front of my colleagues is far more nerve-wracking than delivering it to a room full of strangers. Once I'm comfortable in front of the people I know, I'm confident that I'm ready for the people I don't.

THE HUMOR TRAP

We covered the humor trap more than once, so I won't dwell on it again here. To summarize, don't tell jokes, even of the self-deprecating variety, and don't smile unless you're absolutely sure doing so won't affect your CODE score. In normal situations, humor can be a good way to break the ice and establish rapport with an audience. In tough situations, it almost always sends the wrong signal: that you don't take your audience or their concerns seriously.

THE NEGATIVES TRAP

Being negative is another trap we've covered before. Success comes from being positive ($S = B+$), so whenever possible, convey your stories, messages, and supporting information in a positive way, and approach the conversation or presentation in a positive state of mind. Try to avoid negative words and phrases, particularly when you're answering credibility questions. The occasional "no" or "never" is OK, but if you do use those words, make sure you're not repeating the allegation levied against you:

> *Your Boss:* Did you fail to achieve your goal because you didn't put in enough time?
>
> *You (wrong):* No, I didn't fail because I didn't put in enough time.
>
> *You (right):* On the contrary, I worked harder on this project than anything I've worked on before. Rather than a lack of hard work, I believe the problem was . . .

THE HEDGES TRAP

We use hedges all the time. They typically take the form of a phrase that removes some degree of certainty from a statement:

As far as I know . . .

Well, it really depends.

In my opinion . . .

In normal situations and everyday conversations, hedges are just fine. In fact, they tend to bolster trust and credibility because they suggest a more precise assessment of accuracy. But remember that in tough situations, people perceive everything you say and do through the most negative possible filter. Rather than candor, hedges are interpreted as dishonest and distracting in tough situations.

If you hedge in response to a credibility question from someone who is angry, worried, and suspicious, the questioner will believe you're doing it to give yourself a certain amount of wiggle room. An angry, worried, and suspicious person will conclude that you're not willing to take a firm stand because you're not sure what's really going on—or even worse, you know exactly what's going on but you're trying to hide it from them. (Hedges are OK in response to fact questions when you don't know a precise answer, but try to keep even those to a minimum.)

The best way to avoid the hedge trap or to climb out if you fall in is with certainty and support. Mr. Malone, the power company executive, didn't say, "I think you and your families are safe." He said, "You and your families are safe, and here's why." If you slip up and use a hedge, look for an opportunity to go back and correct your mistake. If you never get the chance, just keep going and avoid using any more hedges.

THE GUARANTEE TRAP

The guarantee trap is particularly tricky, and activists are fond of it. We specifically prepared Mr. Malone for this trap, because we anticipated that someone in his audience would ask whether he could *guarantee* that no one would be harmed by the leak from his power plant. We all know that there are no guarantees in life, so it would seem that you have only two choices when stuck in this trap:

1. Acknowledge there are no guarantees and thereby lead your audience to believe that the risk you're imposing on them is very real and must be resisted at all costs, destroying your CODE score and your ability to win people over; or
2. Make a guarantee that you know you can't back up, which ultimately will subtract openness points from your CODE score, not to mention the possibility—however remote—that you'll get sued.

Fortunately, you have a way to sidestep this trap. Rather than guaranteeing what the questioner has asked, say what you can guarantee:

> *Questioner:* I want a guarantee that my family isn't going to get sick because of the leak from your plant!
>
> *You (wrong):* I think we all know that I can't guarantee that, because there are no guarantees in life.
>
> *You (also wrong):* I can absolutely guarantee that your family won't get sick.

You (right): Let me tell you what I can guarantee you. I can guarantee you that the chances of anyone in your family getting sick are incredibly small. As I've said, I told my own family that they're perfectly safe, and they've been swimming and boating on the lake all summer. I can also guarantee that I will do whatever it takes to prevent something like this from ever happening again. And I guarantee you that we will share everything we learn about this incident with you, so you know exactly what's going on.

THE WORST-CASE SCENARIO TRAP

Also known as the hypothetical trap, the worst-case scenario trap involves making guesses about what might happen if the worst possible scenario were to play out. There's never a good time to engage in that kind of speculation, because it will only make the real risk, whatever it may be, seem that much larger.

The best way to avoid this trap is with a bridge. Several years ago my firm helped to prepare the CEO of a food company to testify before Congress regarding an outbreak of salmonella. His company wasn't responsible for the outbreak, which made several hundred people sick, but he got caught up in the congressional investigation because the outbreak started in one of his customer's facilities. We'll call him Mr. Dawson, because we're going to talk about him again in Chapter 10.

We spent a lot of time rehearsing, particularly answers to several different worst-case scenario questions that we expected. He never got one of those questions, but he was ready for an exchange like the following:

Congressman: Given the amount of tainted meat that got
into the food supply, what's the maximum number of
people who could get sick?

CEO: Congressman, rather than speculate, I think we
should focus on what we know to be true. We know
that about 400 people got sick, and that's unacceptable. Even one case is too many. We know that, fortunately, as far as we know, everyone who got sick has
recovered.

If this trap catches you and you do respond directly to a
hypothetical, try to bridge back to a more specific response as
quickly as you can. This is one of those cases when it's OK to
admit to a mistake by saying something like this:

CEO: You know, I made a mistake responding to a
hypothetical question, and that's an unproductive
exercise that may leave people with the wrong
impression of what happened. I really would prefer
to stick to what we know to be true, which in this
case is . . .

THE DECEPTION/DISHONESTY TRAP

If you fall into the deception/dishonesty trap, it's impossible to
climb out. Once members of an angry, worried, and suspicious
audience decide you're trying to mislead or deceive them or are
outright lying to them, your CODE score will be irreparably
damaged. You might as well pack up your things and go home.
Since you have no way out of this trap, the only recourse you

have is to not fall in. Keep in mind that being deceitful or dishonest is not the same as saying you don't know or making a mistake. Even in a tough situation, people will forgive you as long as you promise to provide an answer or acknowledge or take the time to correct the mistake. This trap involves deliberate deceit or dishonesty, which has no place in breaking through and winning people over under any circumstances.

This trap also will catch you if you try to cover up, which is so often worse than the crime itself. It certainly was for President Clinton, who was impeached not for having an affair with Monica Lewinsky but for lying about it (specifically, perjury and obstruction of justice). Had he simply acknowledged the affair and suffered the embarrassment, he almost certainly would have been spared impeachment. Of course, in President Nixon's case, the crime *was* worse. As I'm writing this chapter, we're in the midst of a controversy over Republican presidential nominee Mitt Romney's decision not to release more than two years' worth of his tax returns. Many are wondering whether he decided that this "cover-up" is preferable to whatever embarrassment he was trying to hide. But it's important to note that no one accused Governor Romney of criminal activity of any kind.

While honesty, as the saying goes, is the best policy, you may find yourself in tough situations where telling the truth isn't so simple (perhaps that was Governor Romney's problem). The truth can be subjective, and even if it's objective, your audience—and your opponents, if they exist—may not accept it anyway. If litigation is a possibility, your attorneys may prohibit you from sharing the whole truth. In these circumstances, you should share as much of the truth as you can and back it up with stories, facts, and data. Be sure to have very good reasons for why you can't share all of the truth, if that's the case. In my firm's experience, legal issues are usually what stand in the way. Fortunately, we've found that audiences, even in tough situations, usually accept the threat of litigation as an acceptable reason for holding back information. If you know when you will be able to share that information, say so and follow up (just as you would if you didn't know the answer).

THE JARGON TRAP

We've discussed jargon already, so there's no need to dwell on it here. Activists love to set this trap. They'll stand up at public meetings and ask jargon-laden questions designed to confuse people who are already angry, worried, and suspicious. Their goal is to erode your CODE score. Don't use jargon yourself, and if someone tries to trap you (or simply asks a question that innocently includes jargon), take the time to define the terms.

Remember, too, that plenty of words and phrases you throw around in everyday conversation may not seem like jargon to you but would to most eighth- or ninth-graders. Even simple business terms such as *fiscal year*, *CEO*, and *stock options* can be confusing to many people and come across as impersonal. Other phrases, including *out-of-the-box thinking* and *new paradigms*, have become clichés as well as jargon.

THE MONEY TRAP

Simply put, the money trap involves placing a price tag on risk. If people believe you're imposing a risk on them, particularly one that threatens their physical well-being, they don't care how much it's going to cost you to eliminate it. If it's going to take $1 billion to make sure that a landfill isn't going to leak, they'll want you to spend $1 billion. If it's going to take $100 billion, they'll want you to spend $100 billion. The same applies to emotional and financial risks. If you have to lay off someone for economic reasons, don't dwell on that aspect of the decision—and definitely don't talk about how much money the organization is going to save by letting her go. Discussing the role that money plays in making decisions makes people feel cheap and undervalued. And it plays into the assumption, which is always present but even more pronounced in tough situations, that people in positions of authority only care about the bottom line.

I slipped partway into this trap myself recently. My firm was a member of an organization that fell on difficult times. The Great Recession took its toll, and by 2012, the organization was losing members and running out of money. Another member of the executive committee and I had to have a difficult conversation with the group's executive director. We weren't sure we were going to make it, and we needed to discuss our options. We started off by talking about the budget and accounts receivable, but it quickly became clear that the executive director wasn't paying attention. She didn't want to hear about money or finances; she was worried about her job. She was thinking, quite understandably, with the emotional part of her brain. So we switched gears and talked about how difficult we knew this was and assured her that our top priority was doing what we could to make sure she was OK. Once we backed up out of the money trap and applied some caring and empathy, the conversation went much more smoothly. (Unfortunately, the organization did not survive. Some outcomes are beyond even the power of the strategies, skills, and techniques contained in this book.)

THE NUMBERS TRAP

Like the dishonesty/deception trap, the numbers trap is one you will not be able to escape once you get caught. This trap falls into the category of risk comparison, which we'll cover in more detail in the next section. It typically comes into play in tough situations that involve public health—the leak from Mr. Malone's power plant, for example. Government agencies and others tend to talk about public health risks in terms of "one out of how many." If a train carrying toxic chemicals derails in this community or that community, how many people out of the entire population will be hurt? One in a thousand? One in ten thousand? We played a little of the numbers game in Chapter 4.

Let me give you an example of how the trap is set. We'll return to the scenario in which one of our clients testified before Congress regarding a salmonella outbreak (though I should point out that, while we prepared for this question, this particular exchange did not take place):

Member of Congress: This outbreak was contained geographically, but let's say we have a nationwide outbreak someday. What are the chances that someone in my district could die as a result?

Client (wrong): Oh, I don't know. It's one in a million.

Member of Congress: One in a million. Well, there are more than 300 million people in this country, right?

Client: Yes, that's right.

Member of Congress: So if I do a little simple math, and assuming you're right about the chances that someone will be killed, that means we can expect 300 people to die during a nationwide salmonella outbreak.

Client: Well, I—

Member of Congress: Is that acceptable to you?

At this point, the client would be caught in the numbers trap and would have no way out.

Avoid this trap by not talking about "one out of how many." Again, use bridges to move from the question to a more appropriate and effective response:

Member of Congress: This outbreak was contained geographically, but let's say we have a nationwide outbreak someday. What are the chances that someone in my district could die as a result?

Client (right): You've raised a hypothetical question, and I can understand why you'd ask it, but I prefer to deal with what we know and can prove . . .

This is also a good place to look for ways to borrow credibility from those who have more than you do. To do that, you would cite an independent source. In this case, regulatory agencies and universities would be particularly effective.

THE RISK COMPARISON TRAP

In Chapter 4, we learned that risk perceptions are influenced by numerous factors that often conspire to turn big risks into nonexistent threats and very small risks into imminent dangers. That makes the use of risk comparisons a dicey proposition, because it's difficult to be sure what your audience perceives to be risky.

Over the years, my firm has had many clients ask if they can compare whatever risk they may be imposing on people with an obvious danger such as smoking or driving. It seems to come up most often with clients that want to build something controversial—a landfill or a power line, for example. They often don't understand why people would protest and resist something like that when they engage in other, much more dangerous behavior on their own. The factors that influence risk that we covered in Chapter 4—trust, benefits, fairness, dread, etc.—explain why.

In this sense, risk comparisons work in much the same way as credibility (see Chapter 2). In tough situations, and normal ones too, it can work to your advantage to borrow credibility from someone who has more than you. But you have to be careful; if the source from whom you're borrowing turns out to have less credibility than you, your own will fall, along with your CODE score.

Similarly, a risk comparison works only if you successfully compare whatever risk you're imposing on others with a risk they *perceive* to be greater, as well as one they believe to be similar. For instance, you might compare driving with riding a train, but definitely not nuclear power with eating peanut butter (which, believe it or not, people in my firm have seen some nuclear engineers try to do). Remember all of the factors that influence risk: control, understanding, benefits, fairness and equity, and so on. Just because something is actually more dangerous than something else does not mean that people perceive it that way. Toxicity also plays a role. Caffeine is more dangerous than plutonium because almost no one will ever be exposed to plutonium, but don't try telling that to the general public. You'll do a lot more harm than good.

Telling someone that the landfill you want to build in their community puts them at less risk than their drive to work every morning will fail (we've seen experts try that, too), because the vast majority of people perceive very little, if any, risk associated with driving and because living near a landfill and driving are not similar activities. You've just compared the risk that you're imposing on them to one they *perceive* to be much lower, which tends to magnify your risk and make their own scarier at the same time. They'll fight the landfill even harder *and* worry a little more on the way home.

Some experts have found that the use of risk comparisons can help put risks in perspective for people when they're angry, worried, and suspicious. They discuss "risk ladders" and "first-rank" and "second-rank" comparisons ordered by desirability. While these concepts are based on sound science, they are complex and difficult to employ without a great deal of skill and practice. My firm counsels clients simply not to use risk comparisons. It's not necessary, and the chances are very high that you'll do more harm than good. If someone specifically asks you to compare risks, use a bridge, with a little caring and empathy thrown in for good measure:

> *Question:* Help us put this in perspective. How does the risk involved compare with, say, the risk of contracting cancer from smoking?
>
> *Response:* I can appreciate that you'd like a little perspective on this. I know I would if I were in your situation, and in fact, my wife asked me exactly the same question. Rather than trying to compare this risk with others, particularly one like smoking and cancer, which is so dangerous and involves so many variables, I think it's more helpful to look at what we're talking about in the following way. . . .

THE FALSE-PREMISE TRAP

Sometimes your audience will try to make an argument based on a false premise. We prepared Mr. Malone, the utility executive, for this trap, because we anticipated that the people in his audience would assume that what his power plant leaked into the lake would be toxic and dangerous. We particularly rehearsed how to respond to the following question:

> *Audience Member:* Since the stuff you leaked in the lake is so dangerous, will you pay for people's medical bills when they get sick?

Mr. Malone's instinct might have been to say something like this:

> *Mr. Malone (wrong):* The leak is not dangerous, and you won't get sick, so there's no point in talking about medical bills.

But that breaks too many of our rules. It's not very caring and empathetic. It also includes too many negatives and repeats the allegation. Here's what we counseled Mr. Malone to say if that question came up (which it didn't):

> *Mr. Malone (right):* I appreciate that question. I'm sure many other people are wondering the same thing. Let's step back for a minute. As I said, the leak was very small, and we have been unable to detect any traces of it since the moments after it happened. You and your family are perfectly safe. You can swim and fish without any concern. Medical bills won't be an issue.

Another form of the false-premise trap involves a forced alternative:

> *Audience Member:* Isn't it best just to shut the plant down so we can be sure this will never happen again?
>
> *Audience Member:* Shouldn't we ban swimming and fishing in the lake just to be sure?

The best response to these questions is something like this:

Mr. Malone: I hear what you're saying, and I too want to
make sure everyone is safe. As I said, my family lives
here, and my grandchildren often swim in the lake.
But the actions you suggest are unnecessary, and your
family is safe. The leak was small and undetectable,
and people should feel free to enjoy the lake as they
always have.

In either case, the way out of the trap is the same: express
caring and empathy, deny the false premise or forced alternative
in a positive way, and bridge to one of your messages.

In my firm's experience, these are the most common traps you're
likely to encounter. Apply the strategies, skills, and techniques
we've covered in this book, and you should be able to avoid any
others you may come across. If some do ensnare you, you should
be able to escape.

Now that you know what to avoid, let's look at a model
my firm has developed for answering any question in a tough
situation.

Chapter 10

THE CAN RESPONSE

Yes we can!

—BARACK OBAMA, CANDIDATE

W e've covered a lot of ground over the previous nine chapters, and your head may be spinning just a little. How am I supposed to remember to express caring and empathy while keeping my hands visible? What signal do I send if I look up and to the right? Which portion of my CODE score should I try to bolster if I'm a man? At what grade level am I supposed to aim my messages? Should I wear a tie?

If you feel that way, it's perfectly normal. At some point during their training, almost all the people with whom I work worry that they'll never remember to do everything right or be able to earn a perfect CODE score. As with any skill, the ability to break through and win people over must be built over time through lots and lots of practice. This book will give you a strong foundation on which to build. Hopefully, you'll keep it on a shelf in your office and review it from time to time, especially before you're about to engage in a conversation with someone who's angry, worried, and suspicious.

In this chapter, we're going to review another tool you can use to pull together many of the strategies, skills, and techniques we've discussed. My firm calls it the CAN Response (hence my use of Barack Obama's campaign slogan as opening quote for this chapter), and it provides a framework for answering the most difficult questions people ask in tough situations. I've referred to these as credibility questions—questions that directly challenge your trust and credibility and are designed to drive down your CODE score (unlike fact questions, which are meant to elicit basic information and are not aimed at your CODE score). Credibility questions come in many forms. Here are some of the most common ones:

- ▶ Why should I trust you?
- ▶ Are you lying to me?
- ▶ Why should I believe you?
- ▶ Why are you doing this to me?
- ▶ What are you going to do about the harm you've caused me?

When someone asks a credibility question like one of these, alarm bells should go off in your head. Remember, your first priority in a tough situation is to establish and maintain trust and credibility. If you don't, you will never be able to win people over when they're angry, worried, and suspicious of everything you say. A credibility question is a signal that your CODE score is under attack, and you need to do everything you can to keep it as close to 100 as possible.

The CAN Response is a simple, straightforward model for answering credibility questions. To see how it works, let's break it down letter by letter.

C Is for Caring

The CAN Response begins with a *C* for the same reason that the CODE for trust and credibility begins with a *C*: caring and empathy together are the most important criterion by which people judge whether or not you're a trustworthy and credible person and source of information. When you're answering a credibility question, the first words out of your mouth must be caring and empathetic. Again, the best way to do this is to tell a personal story that resonates with your audience.

Remember Mr. Dawson from the previous chapter? He's the food company CEO we helped to prepare for testimony before a congressional committee regarding a salmonella outbreak. We anticipated that one of the members of the committee would accuse him of making people sick. He might also hear the same thing from reporters or regulators—or even from someone who got sick. We had to make sure he was ready for that accusation.

It turned out that Mr. Dawson had suffered from food poisoning during an overseas trip, so we encouraged him to talk about that experience when it felt appropriate. I'm paraphrasing (and I'm not sure he ever had to use the anecdote), but it went something like this:

I can sure understand why you would be worried and upset about getting sick. Food poisoning is scary. It actually happened to me about five years ago during a trip abroad. I was sick as a dog for two days. Fortunately, it passed pretty quickly, and all I missed was a couple of days of vacation. But when I got back, I redoubled my efforts to make sure my company does everything possible to ensure that its products and processes are safe, because I don't ever want anyone to feel the way I did.

Remember that men need to spend more time expressing caring and empathy than women. A full CAN Response should last between two and three minutes. For men, about one-third of the response (between 40 and 60 seconds) should be devoted to the *C* in CAN. Women can limit caring and empathy to about one-fifth of the answer, or about 30 seconds. In either case, the only way to fill that much time is with a personal story.

People often ask me if they need to express that much caring and empathy in response to every single question. The answer is no. It's important to do so initially, when your audience is first judging whether or not you're trustworthy and credible. When you begin to sense that you've earned all 50 caring and empathy points, you can start to back off from expressing caring and empathy every time someone asks you a question, especially if it is a fact question. But keep the *C* in mind. If things are going well and then someone suddenly fires a tough credibility question at you, go back to basics and provide a full CAN Response that includes a complete dose of caring and empathy right up front.

A Is for Answer

Once you've provided the right amount of caring and empathy, the next step is to answer the question. The whole point of establishing trust and credibility is so you can impart information that will change people's attitudes and beliefs. If the *C* of a CAN Response is the part that allows you to break through to people, the *A* is the part where you win them over. We don't necessarily want people who are angry, worried, and suspicious to remember that you're trustworthy and credible, although that's what you need to be. As we discussed in Chapter 3, what we want them to remember are your key messages. The *A* represents the portion of your CAN Response where you convey that message, or sound bite.

The formula for the *A* portion of your CAN Response is:

message-supporting facts-message

Let's take a closer look at each element of this formula.

Message

Let's visit with Mr. Malone from Chapter 5 one more time. He very effectively used just about every strategy, skill, and technique we've discussed, and he earned a CODE score of close to 100. But Mr. Malone didn't want the people in the auditorium to remember how caring he was. Or open. Or dedicated. Instead, he wanted them to remember that the leak, while unfortunate, was very small and that it would not harm them or their families. In fact, the answer to most credibility questions is often some variation of, "You're going to be OK." The message

Mr. Malone was trying to send was, "You and your family are safe." Dr. Pierce from Chapter 4 wanted people to know that the procedure he was defending was "safe, effective, and necessary." If you're encouraging an employee to improve his performance, it might be "While we need you to step up your game, we want you to do well here."

Whatever its content, your sound bite message should be:

▶ *Short and simple.* Since the message is what you want people to remember, you need to make it *easy* to remember. A long message containing big words won't work. Keep it to between 7 and 12 words, and leave out any jargon. Try to use words with no more than three syllables; two is even better.

▶ *Positive.* Do your best to eliminate negative words from your answers. It's always possible to flip a message to make it positive. Note that Mr. Malone didn't say, "Don't worry about the leak." If someone asks why you're lying to her, don't respond by saying, "I'm not lying to you." Try "I'm telling you the truth" instead. If you're arguing with a significant other, it's "I need you to hear what I'm saying," rather than "You're not listening to me."

▶ *Caring and empathetic.* Many of the people I train have trouble distinguishing between a message and a fact. Since so much of what we work on involves caring and empathy, it usually helps them to think that way when formulating the *A* part of their CAN Responses. Mr. Malone didn't want people to remember that the leak was small or that it had dissipated to below background exposure levels.

The professor who joined him on the stage that night sent those kinds of messages, and the audience attacked him. The message you convey should not be factual; it should be caring: "You're going to be OK," not "Exposure levels are too low to cause harm." Ultimately, the answer portion of your response must address the underlying concern contained in the question. In most cases, that underlying concern will involve fears about personal safety or well-being. Occasionally it will involve financial concerns or emotional burdens. Every time, the messages you convey should address those fears.

Supporting Facts

The message is only the first part of the *A*. Once you've conveyed the message, you need to support it. Almost by definition, messages are assertions. If you want someone to process and believe them, you need to back them up. This is where you want to include supporting facts that help to prove that the assertion contained in your message is true.

The second part of your answer should include two supporting facts. Remember the power of third-party credibility, and try to use one fact that cites an independent expert with greater credibility than you. Had the professor's CODE score not been so low because of his own mistakes, Mr. Malone could have cited him as a credible independent expert. The other supporting fact can be almost anything, although a good, short anecdote is most effective. The same rules that we applied to the message portion of the answer also apply to the supporting facts: keep them short, simple, and (if possible) caring and empathetic.

Message Again

Once you've provided your supporting facts, repeat the message (or sound bite) exactly as you stated it at the beginning. Repetition is the basis for any good ad campaign, because people need to hear or see something at least several times before it really penetrates.

We even encourage our clients to highlight the message somehow. One way is to raise your voice slightly while conveying the message, so people hear it more clearly and understand that it's more important than everything else you're saying. Another is to telegraph the message verbally by saying something like "Here's the most important thing I'm going to say to you" or "If you only remember one thing I've said, this is it." The goal is to make sure the message penetrates.

N Is for Next Steps

Before you complete a CAN Response, you should make one last effort to boost your CODE score by letting your audience know what's going to come next. This is all about the *D* in CODE, or dedication. If you're reprimanding an employee, let him know what you intend to do to fix the situation. Tell him, for example, that you're going to meet twice a week at a certain day and time to review his performance. Encourage him to come to you if he has any questions or concerns. If you're talking to a group of people, copy Mr. Malone and bring business cards to hand out so they can reach you after the meeting is over. Or make sure everyone has your e-mail address.

Provide sources where audience members can go to get more information. Borrow credibility as often as you can by offering third-party sources (in today's world, websites are the best ones), as well as your own. This is also the place to reiterate that you'll get back to people with answers to the questions you didn't know.

Samples to Help Get You Started

While every CAN Response follows the same pattern, each one will be different. As you prepare to communicate in a tough situation, you need to think about the credibility questions you're likely to get and prepare CAN Responses for each one. Here are three full CAN Responses to demonstrate how the model works.

Scenario 1: Testifying Before Congress

Mr. Dawson appears before the House Subcommittee on Livestock, Dairy, and Poultry to answer questions about the salmonella outbreak involving his company. The chairman asks the following question: "Mr. Dawson, what do you have to say to the people who got sick and to their families?"

> C: Mr. Chairman, I know firsthand how uncomfortable
>   and scary it can be to suffer from food poisoning. It
>   actually happened to me about five years ago during
>   a trip abroad. I ate dinner one night, and the meal
>   seemed like it was properly prepared and perfectly safe.
>   As it turned out, three hours later, I was sick as a dog.
>   I didn't leave my hotel for two days. It was awful, but

fortunately it passed pretty quickly. Ultimately, all I lost was a couple of days of vacation. I know that many of the people affected by this outbreak have suffered much worse. A handful of people have been hospitalized, but, thankfully, I understand that everyone is expected to recover. My heart goes out to them, and I'm very pleased that they're all going to be OK.

I take my responsibilities as the CEO of my company very seriously, and I recognize that in my position, I have the ability to do something about food safety. When I was sick in that hotel room, I vowed to redouble my efforts to make sure our company's processes and products are safe, because I don't ever want anyone to feel the way I did. This is the first time in the five years since that day that my company has come under scrutiny for a food poisoning incident.

A: We've conducted a thorough investigation of our facilities, and my message to you, Mr. Chairman, and to the rest of this committee and to all of our customers is the following:

The salmonella in this incident came from somewhere other than our company.

Our investigation involved our own experts as well as officials from the U.S. Department of Agriculture and the state Department of Food Safety. These experts reached this unanimous conclusion after spending more than a month inspecting our facilities and talking to our suppliers and our customers.

I recognize that our findings provide little comfort to those who were affected by this outbreak. Even one incident of food poisoning, regardless of the source, is too many. I know I didn't really care why or how I got sick on my trip. I just wanted to feel better. But it is important for me to say this to you and to our customers, once again:

The salmonella in this incident came from somewhere other than our company.

N: Even if it came from somewhere else, we still take this outbreak very seriously. I have formed a special task force in our company to review all of our policies and procedures to determine what else we can do make sure that our company provides safe, affordable, and nutritious products.

Everyone has a role to play in safe food preparation. Consumers should follow all the proper guidelines when preparing their food. To help, my company has created a special website where our customers can go to learn how to prepare all of our different products safely. I also pledge to you and to our customers today that when the special task force's review is complete, we will share what we learned and whatever steps we're taking on that website.

Scenario 2: Terminating an Employee

You have to let an employee go for poor performance. After you deliver the bad news, she asks, "Why are you doing this to me?"

C: I know how hard this is. It happened to me when I was about your age. I took a job that I didn't really even want, because I needed it. And it wasn't a good fit right from the very beginning. I tried, but I wasn't all that interested in the job or the work. I knew I wasn't doing as good a job as I could. My boss told me several times that I needed to improve my performance or he would have to let me go, just as we've talked two or three times about your performance here.

Eventually, he called me into his office and told me my time had run out. Even though I knew it was coming, I was still shocked. And I was embarrassed. I didn't want to tell anyone, and I left the building in a state of shock. This was more than 20 years ago, but I still remember how it felt.

Now here's the good news: Even though it didn't feel like it at the time, now I see how getting laid off from that job was the best thing that ever happened to me. After I got over the initial shock, I went back to school and got my master's degree and wound up pursuing a completely different career. Now here I am in a job that I really love, and I'm much happier.

A: And here's what I want you to remember as you leave here today:

You're going to be just fine.

I looked it up before you came in here, and more than half of the people working today have lost at least one job at some point during their careers. It's very common.

Let's just chalk this up to a bad fit. I'm sure you can't see it now, but one day you'll look back, just as I did, and realize that this is the best thing that ever happened to you. So again, my main message to you is this:

You're going to be just fine.

N: We're going to provide you with a month's severance, and you can stay on our health insurance plan for nine months. We'll pay the premiums for the first three, and then they'll become your responsibility. And I want you to take my card with you. While this job may not have been a good fit, I like you personally, and I know you're going to land on your feet. Call me anytime if you need some advice or some help, and please let me know when you've found a new job.

Scenario 3: Defending a Change

You head a professional society that represents thousands of people, and you decide to adopt a new logo for the first time in 25 years. Many of your members have a very strong affinity for the old logo. When you announce the change at your annual convention, several members ask, "Why are you replacing something that everyone knows so well?"

C: Change is always hard, especially when it comes to something as important as a logo. I can tell you have a lot invested in what we have today; so do I. I see that logo every day in our lobby when I arrive in the morning. It's on all the checks I sign. It's on my business card. Everywhere I look, there it is. It may sound a little corny, but that logo has become a part of who I am. So I understand completely why you're asking that question. When we first started talking about developing a new logo, I asked myself the very same thing. And I talked to a lot of people before we decided to move forward. I always asked them "Are we thinking about fixing something that isn't broken?"

A: Here's what I usually heard in response, and it's the best way to answer your question:

Our current logo *is* broken, and we need to change it if we want to grow and thrive.

That's so important that I want to say it one more time:

Our current logo is broken, and we need to change it if we want to grow and thrive.

Here's why I say that. We recently did a survey of our members, and more than 60 percent said the current logo no longer represents what our organization has become. Roughly the same number said it was time for a change. The percentages were even higher among emerging professionals who have been members for less than five years. Those survey findings helped to convince me that the time had come for change.

What really affected my thinking was a conversation I had about six months ago with a recent college graduate in our field. When I suggested that he consider joining our organization, he told me that he already had considered it but decided not to. He looked at our website and talked to one of his professors, and based on what he learned, he decided we just weren't relevant to his career. I realize it's only one person's opinion, but his decision really resonated with me. So when I asked myself the question you just asked me, again, here's my answer:

Our current logo is broken, and we need to change if we want to grow and thrive.

N: So I believe that this new logo is a very important step for us, but it really represents the beginning. We need to roll out the logo and implement a real branding strategy that will prove to people that we're a different organization and that they should take another look. I plan to send it to that student with just that recommendation.

In the meantime, we need your help. We know this process will be successful only if we have our members' support. I'm eager to hear what you think about it and how you think we can best make the transition. I'd like to know what challenges you think we'll face. Feel free to grab me any time during this meeting. We've also set up a special e-mail address where you can send thoughts and feedback: newlogo@ourorg .org. You'll also see a new LinkedIn discussion group on the topic, and I'm sure this will become a major topic on our online forum.

MASTERING THE CAN RESPONSE

While each of these scenarios is based on real situations in which I've been involved, I did take a few liberties with the details included in these CAN Responses. Obviously, when you're preparing your CAN Responses, every word you say has to be true and sincere (openness and honesty provide 15 to 20 points of your CODE score, after all). Once you have the formula down, constructing CAN Responses will become second nature.

Delivering a full CAN Response typically takes two to three minutes. As Figure 10.1 illustrates, one advantage of that length is that you can get out a full response in a single breath—although that takes extra practice and skill.

FIGURE 10.1 Take a Deep Breath

When the stakes are really high, it's helpful to learn how to deliver the entire CAN Response without breathing. Why? If you don't breathe, your audience is much less likely to interrupt you. It also becomes important for people who agree to interviews with *60 Minutes* and other big-time television news programs. If you don't breathe, it's very difficult for a reporter or producer to edit your answer and air only part of it. The show has to air either the whole thing, including the all-important caring and empathy, or nothing at all.

©iStockphoto.com/jdavidlong

As complicated as it may seem, the CAN Response is pretty basic. Vincent Covello teaches a more complex model that he calls the Level 6 Response. By that measure, the CAN Response is more like Level 3 or 4. While the formula is essentially the same, the Level 6 Response is longer—closer to three and a half or four minutes—and consists of 17 different parts. And then there's the Level 10 Response, which is a Level 6 done without breathing.

Finally, remember: practice makes perfect. Once you've prepared your CAN Responses, try them out on a colleague or family member. I've always found that when I can perform well in front of people I know and who trust me, I'm ready to communicate with people when they're angry, worried, and suspicious of everything I say.

CONCLUSION

I'm sure that as you read through this book, you thought about tough situations you've been in and some of the angry, worried, and suspicious people you've had to win over. I hope you've learned some things that will drive up your CODE score the next time.

As a consultant, I don't find myself having to break through and win people over in tough situations very often; usually, I'm off to the side, counseling, preparing, and training my clients to do so. It does happen from time to time. The story I told at the beginning of Chapter 2—and used as a model CAN response in Chapter 10—about helping the professional society unveil its new name, logo, and tagline is a good example. Because my firm led the effort to develop the new brand concept, the client asked me (and one of my colleagues) to present it. I wore a suit, one step above anyone else in the room. I told a story with a nice arc that described how we overcame adversity and triumphed in the end. While the organization forced me to stand behind a lectern, I made sure my hands were visible. I planted my feet and leaned into the audience. I did use PowerPoint, but I included just a few slides with very few words (mostly, I used the program to unveil the new logo and tagline).

Let me share one more example, this time from my personal life, that often reminds me of just how powerful these strategies, skills, and techniques can be.

Easily the toughest communication situation I ever faced was when my ex-wife and I had to tell our two kids that we had decided to divorce. While I understood that a life-changing conversation like that differs dramatically from telling someone that they're fired or helping a client defend the construction of a landfill, I also realized that, in many ways, I was about to enter a tough situation—a tough situation in which I was imposing an enormous emotional burden on an audience that very quickly would become angry and worried, if not a little suspicious. So I carefully prepared what I was going to say, and I rehearsed many times with my ex-wife, members of my family, and even a family friend who happened to be a psychiatrist.

At the time, my daughter was 7, and my son was 11. My ex-wife and I sat down with them in the living room of our house, and I broke the news in a reassuring voice as gently as I could. Then I told them this story:

When I was 11 and my brother was 7, the same age as they were, my parents decided to move from Cleveland to Fort Lauderdale. It was the right decision for our family; my dad's job in Ohio was precarious at the time, and he landed a great new one in Florida. But it was very hard on us kids. I didn't want to leave all my friends in Cleveland, and I felt powerless because I couldn't do anything to change what was happening to me. The sensation was similar to walking through water, feeling constrained and confused and unable to move. I don't make friends easily, so the idea that I would have to find new ones was particularly daunting. I'd be living in a brand-new house and going to a brand-new school. Everything about it was scary.

But, as I told my kids that cold, crisp, sunny November morning, eventually I made new friends and came to like my new school and even wound up serving as the president of my senior class in high school. It was a hard transition, but in the end, I wound up just fine.

And that's the message I conveyed to my kids: I know this is scary, but just like me, you're going to be fine.

Then I told them that it wasn't their fault, that Mommy and Daddy wanted each other to be happy, and that what we cared about more than anything else was them and their well-being. I explained that I was going to move out of the house and get a new apartment nearby, and that they would be spending half their time with me and half their time with their mom. They'd still go to the same schools and see their friends and spend time with both sides of the families. And then I repeated my message: I know this is scary, but just like me, you're going to be fine.

We asked them if they had any questions. My son didn't say anything. All my daughter wanted to know was if we could still go to the mall, as we had promised her the night before. So we went to the mall.

If I've done my job right over the course of this book's 10 chapters, you immediately recognized the CAN Response model in the script I used to tell my kids about our divorce. I know it helped me organize my thoughts and share this unbelievably difficult information in the most caring, empathetic, dedicated, open, honest, and expert way possible. I think it helped them process it, even at the young ages of 7 and 11. In the months and years that followed, they never expressed any anger about their "new normal," and they never complained, not once. They accepted and adjusted to this massive life change, much bigger than the one I had experienced when my brother and I were their ages, with grace and fortitude. Now they're 14 and 18, and they're terrific, well-adjusted kids. And that is why, if you read this book's dedication, I consider them to be the two most courageous people I know.

THE THREE MESSAGES I WANT YOU TO REMEMBER

Along the way, I mentioned the power of repetition, so I'm going to take a page out of my own book (so to speak) and repeat what I believe to be the three most important messages I tried to convey and hope have come through loud and clear. Since you've now been exposed to the concept of a message triangle, let me use that device for my own purposes. Figure C.1 shows the "breaking through and winning people over" message triangle that I use to close my training presentations.

IT'S ALL ABOUT TRUST AND CREDIBILITY

Everything we've discussed in the preceding pages is aimed at driving your CODE score as close to 100 as possible, because that means you've built the maximum amount of trust and credibility with your audience. You have to achieve that objective

FIGURE C.1 The "Breaking Through and Winning People Over" Message Triangle

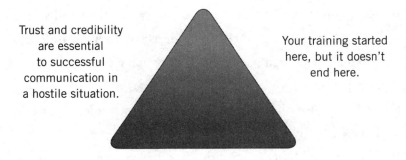

Trust and credibility
are essential
to successful
communication in
a hostile situation.

Your training started
here, but it doesn't
end here.

Communicating in tough situations is more art
than science, and doing it well requires a lot of
practice, preparation, and rehearsal.

A message triangle is a great way to organize the three most important points you want to make in any situation, tough or otherwise. This is a message triangle containing the three most important points I intended to make in this book. Feel free to make a copy and tape it to your desk or computer screen, and refer to it any time you're about to face a tough situation.

before you can hope to change people's attitudes, actions, and beliefs. Another way to think about it is that people have to like you before they will listen to you. In normal situations, the people with whom we communicate already like us. Family, friends, colleagues—we've earned their trust and credibility. In tough situations, that's not the case. People are preprogrammed to dislike and distrust us, because they believe we're imposing some sort of risk on them and don't have their best interests at heart.

To build and maintain trust and credibility in tough situations, you have to send all the right verbal and nonverbal messages. That means you need to:

▶ Remember that when people are angry, worried, and suspicious of everything you say, emotions trump facts. Indeed, too many facts can backfire and only make your audience angrier and more worried and suspicious.

▶ Tell your story in the most positive way possible, using the fewest negative words and phrases.

▶ Borrow credibility from those who have more than you, in order to support the messages you're trying to convey (and being careful not to borrow credibility from someone with less than you, which will only drive down your own).

▶ Eliminate jargon—every word or phrase that an eighth- or ninth-grader wouldn't know—from your vocabulary, and define any jargon you're forced to use.

▶ Tell simple, brief, honest, and compelling stories that resonate with the people you're trying to win over and that convey the messages you're trying to send—without using PowerPoint or any other presentation software to help you tell them.

▶ Understand that people become angry, worried, and suspicious of everything you say because they believe you're imposing a risk on them; that the risks people fear and the risks that most threaten them are usually very different; and that many different factors influence how people perceive, assess, and ultimately accept risk.

▶ Keep in mind the four criteria that play into how people decide whether or not you're a trustworthy and credible source of information and that make up your CODE score: caring, openness, dedication, and expertise. Apply all the strategies, skills, and techniques that can help you drive your score to 100.

▶ Pay careful attention to the nonverbal messages you send with your eyes, hands, posture, dress, and arrival and departure, as well as any physical barriers that stand between you and your audience.

▶ Remember that men and women enter tough situations with different initial CODE scores, because people perceive men to be more expert but women to be more caring, open, and dedicated. Employ different strategies to boost your CODE score based on your gender.

▶ Understand the context in which today's media operate. Direct your stories and messages at the audiences you're trying to win over, rather than the reporter with whom you're talking. Employ all the strategies, skills, and techniques necessary to break through in interviews—especially bridging from the question you've been asked to the messages you want to convey.

▶ Avoid and, when necessary, escape from the most common traps that may trip you up in tough situations.

▶ Develop CAN Responses to the credibility questions you expect your audience to ask—for the easy questions as well as the hard ones.

This Is the Beginning of Your Training, Not the End

As I said in the Preface, reading this book will not immediately make you an expert at breaking through and winning people over when they're angry, worried, and suspicious of everything you say. While it has provided you with strategies, skills, and techniques that will get you started, now you have to spend time building on the basic foundation we've laid here. Even the greatest communicators of all time weren't born that way. In Chapter 3, I named Franklin Roosevelt, Ronald Reagan, and Martin Luther King Jr. as being among the twentieth century's best storytellers. Although most of them did possess a lot of natural talent, they developed and perfected their skills over many years before stepping onto the national stage: Roosevelt during a long political career that included service as a state senator and governor of New York; Reagan as an actor, pitchman for General Electric, and governor of California; and King as a minister and longtime civil rights activist.

While I tried to make this book as practical as possible, reading and understanding the stories I shared about my firm's work is very different from actually standing in front of a group of angry, worried, and suspicious people. It's always a great experience for me to be the one onstage and in the line of fire, because it gives me a sense of what my clients face, and it makes me a better consultant. It also provides me with stories I can relate in a caring and empathetic way. I think I've acquitted myself well in these situations, but I know that even my own skills are not as polished as I'd like them to be—or that yours can be.

It's very important that you work with your organization's communications professionals before you step into a tough situation. And not to sound too self-serving, but regular training with a consultant like me can be a great way to reinforce what we covered in the book and to build on your skills. That leads to my final message:

YOU'RE PERFORMING ON A STAGE

As with any other skill, the only way to get better at breaking through and winning people over is to practice, prepare, and rehearse. Since, for most of us, tough situations are (thankfully) rare, we don't get many chances to go onstage for a real, live performance, as professional actors or athletes do. So that puts a real premium on rehearsal. That's relatively easy to do when you have advance notice of a tough situation. You can take all of the steps we've discussed: consider your audience, line up your stories, settle on your messages, think about questions (both easy and hard), and so on. Before you go onstage, grab a friend or colleague, and engage in a mock exercise that's as real as you can make it. Make sure your practice partner knows enough to be as tough on you as your audience will be.

Crises, by definition, arise without warning. You can do a lot of planning and preparation for those, too, but that's a subject for an entirely different book. I encourage my clients and trainees to run drills from time to time, even when no tough situations are on the horizon. Make one up, or use the last one you faced as a model. Run through all the steps, including a dress rehearsal in front of a "live" audience. That will help to keep your skills honed.

Since I opened with a quote from a football coach, I'll close with one as well, this time from Vince Lombardi:

Practice does not make perfect. Only perfect practice makes perfect.

Be positive, and break a leg!

RECOMMENDED READING

For readers who are interested in more information about the strategies, skills, and techniques we've covered in this book or about similar topics, I offer the following list of sources.

Brehove, Aaron. *Body Language: Techniques on Interpreting Nonverbal Cues in the World and Workplace.* Guilford, CT: Morris Book Publishing, 2011.

Eckman, Paul. *Emotion in the Human Face*, 3rd ed. New York: Oxford University Press, 2007.

Fischer, Roger, William Ury, and Bruce Patton. *Getting to Yes: Negotiating Agreement Without Giving In.* New York: Penguin Group, 2011.

Kinsley Goman, Carol. *The Nonverbal Advantage: Secrets and Science of Body Language at Work.* San Francisco: Berrett-Koehler Publishers, 2008.

Lumsden, Gary, and Donald Lumsden. *Communicating with Credibility and Confidence: Diverse People, Diverse Settings,* 2nd ed. Belmont, CA: Wadsworth/Thompson Learning, 2003.

Mehrabian, Albert. *Silent Messages: Implicit Communication of Emotions and Attitudes*, 2nd ed. Belmont, CA: Wadsworth Publishing, 1980.

National Research Council, Committee on Risk Perception and Communication. *Improving Risk Communication*. Washington, DC: National Research Council, 1989.

Patterson, Kerry, et al. *Crucial Confrontations: Tools for Resolving Broken Promises, Violated Expectations, and Bad Behavior.* New York: McGraw-Hill, 2005.

———. *Crucial Conversations: Tools for Talking When Stakes Are High*, 2nd ed. New York: McGraw-Hill, 2012.

Pettinelli, Mark. *The Psychology of Emotions, Feelings and Thoughts*, 4th ed. Mark Pettinelli, 2008.

Ropeik, David, and George Gray. *Risk: A Practical Guide for Deciding What's Really Safe and What's Really Dangerous in the World Around You.* Boston: Houghton Mifflin, 2002.

Sandman, Peter M. "The Peter M. Sandman Risk Communication Website." http://www.psandman.com/.

Stone, Douglas, Bruce Patton, and Sheila Heen. *Difficult Conversations: How to Discuss What Matters Most.* New York: Penguin Group, 1999.

Tymson, Candy. *Gender Games: Doing Business with the Opposite Sex.* Milsons Point, New South Wales: Tymson Communications, 1998.

Works Cited

Introduction

P. xxxiii Miranda, Christina, "Five tips to deliver bad news gracefully." *The Voice of Reason in Marketing* blog at http://redpointspeak.com, August 29, 2012.

P. xvii Wingo, Hal C., "Re: The Transition." *New Yorker* (letter to the editor), April 23, 2012.

Chapter 1: The Science Behind the Art

P. 4 "The application of risk communication to food standards and safety matters," Report of a Joint United Nations Food and Agriculture Organization/World Health Organization Expert Consultation, Rome, February 2–6, 1998, p. 3.

P. 6 Wolbarst, Anthony. *Solutions to an Environment in Peril.* Baltimore: The Johns Hopkins University Press, 2001. Chapter 15, "Risk Communication: Evolution and Revolution," by Vincent T. Covello and Peter M. Sandman.

P. 8 "Seven Cardinal Rules of Risk Communication," drafted by Vincent T. Covello, Frederick W. Allen, et al, and published by the *U.S. Environmental Protection Agency*, April 1988.

Chapter 2: Laying the Foundation

P. 18 Pettinelli, Mark. *The Psychology of Emotions, Feelings and Thoughts*, 4th ed. Mark Pettinelli, 2008.

P. 28 "U.S. Distrust in Media Hits New High," press release issued by Gallup, September 21, 2012.

P. 29 *Nielsen Global Trust in Advertising Survey*, The Nielsen Company, April 2012.

CHAPTER 3: THE LOST ART OF STORYTELLING

P. 36 Koerth-Baker, Maggie, "The Mind of a Flip-Flopper." *New York Times Magazine*, August 15, 2012.

CHAPTER 4: REAL RISK VS. PERCEIVED RISK, OR WHY WE DRIVE

P. 41 "The Washington sniper," case study by the Centre of Risk for Health Care Research and Practice. http://www.smd.qmul.ac.uk/risk/yearone/casestudies/washington-sniper.html

P. 52 Ropeik, David, and George Gray. *Risk: A Practical Guide for Deciding What's Really Safe and What's Really Dangerous in the World Around You.* Boston: Houghton Mifflin, 2002.

P. 56 Slovic, Paul, "Perception of risk." *Science*, April 17, 1987.

P. 58 "New Allstate Survey Shows Americans Think They Are Great Drivers—Habits Tell a Different Story," press release by Allstate Insurance, August 2, 2011.

CHAPTER 5: THE CODE FOR TRUST AND CREDIBILITY

P. 77 Peters, Richard G., Vincent T. Covello and David B. McCallum, "The Determinants of Trust and Credibility in Environmental Risk Communication: An Empirical Study." *Risk Analysis*, 1997; 17(1).

P. 79 Witt, P. L., Brown, K. C., Roberts, J. B., Weisel, J., Sawyer, C. R., & Behnke, R. R., "Somatic anxiety patterns of student speakers before, during, and after giving a public speech." *Southern Communication Journal*, March 2006; vol. 71.

P. 81 Stone, Douglas, Bruce Patton, and Sheila Heen. *Difficult Conversations: How to Discuss What Matters Most.* New York: Penguin Group, 1999.

CHAPTER 6: NONVERBAL MESSAGES AND THEIR IMPACT ON THE CODE

P. 101 Kinsley Goman, Carol. *The Nonverbal Advantage: Secrets and Science of Body Language at Work.* San Francisco: Berrett-Koehler Publishers, 2008.

P. 108 Ekman, Paul. *Emotion in the Human Face*, 3rd ed. New York: Oxford University Press, 2007.

P. 110 Tecce, J. J., "Body Language," Unpublished, February 2009 http://www.theblaze.com/blog/2012/10/04/and-now-a-debate -analysis-of-obamas-blinking-habits/.

CHAPTER 7: THE CREDIBILITY GENDER GAP

P. 134 Tymson, Candy. *Gender Games: Doing Business with the Opposite Sex.* Milsons Point, New South Wales: Tymson Communications, 1998.

P. 134 Sedacca, Rosalind, "Helping Business Women Bridge the Gender Communication Gap." *EXPERT Magazine*, June 30, 2002.

CHAPTER 8: MASTERING THE MEDIA

P. 142 Zakaria, Fareed, presentation to the American Society of Association Executives Annual Meeting in Toronto, August 2009.

P. 143 *The State of the News Media 2012*, The Pew Research Center's Project for Excellence in Journalism, March 2012.

P. 145 History Channel, 2000.

P. 146 *The State of the News Media 2012*, The Pew Research Center's Project for Excellence in Journalism, March 2012.

P. 156 Appearance on *This Week with George Stephanopoulos*, ABC News, August 29, 2004.

CHAPTER 9: AVOIDING AND ESCAPING TRAPS

P. 174 Keller, Carmen. "Using a familiar risk comparison within a risk ladder to improve risk understanding by low numerates: a study of visual attention." *Risk Analysis*, July 2011; 31(7).

INDEX

About the Author

Leonard S. Greenberger works with hundreds of clients—including senior corporate and nonprofit executives and military officers—to prepare them to communicate in tough situations. He is a seasoned veteran of guiding clients through crises where effective communication often makes the difference between success and failure.

As a partner at Potomac Communications Group (PCG) in Washington, D.C., where he has worked for more than 20 years, he helped to adapt the firm's study of risk perception and assessment into a training curriculum that teaches the strategies, skills, and techniques necessary to win people over when they are angry, worried, and suspicious. He and the firm also expanded the application of the curriculum beyond areas involving traditional environmental risks to everyday business situations, from branding to employee relations.

Leonard earned a bachelor of arts in communications at the University of Michigan and a master of science in journalism from the Medill School of Journalism at Northwestern University. Prior to joining PCG, he covered Capitol Hill for an energy industry trade magazine. He has presented and written extensively on communicating in challenging situations for a variety of audiences, public and private, and consumer and trade publications. *What to Say When Things Get Tough* is his first, but hopefully not last, book.

An avid runner and reader, Leonard lives in Washington, D.C., with his two children. He can be reached at lgreenberger @pcgpr.com.